T0265205

All Eyes and Blind

Parable Stories for Sunday Scriptures
—Cycle B—

Francis Patrick Sullivan

Sheed & Ward

Sheed & Ward™ is a service of National Catholic Reporter Publishing
Company Inc.

Library of Congress Catalog Card Number: 90-61960

ISBN: 1-55612-354-X

Published by: Sheed & Ward
                115 E. Armour Blvd. P.O. Box 419492
                Kansas City, MO 64141-4292

To order, call: (800) 333-7373

Contents

A.M.D.G.

Preface

The stories in this book can be used to gain insight into scripture, either the meaning scripture has, or the meaning it lacks. The process is classical which seeks the relationship between ancient texts and life in later time. The relationship is like a conversation, not like a submission, so that mutual illumination occurs, not alienation.

A preacher will find a sense in each story that follows, a sense that had to be struggled for by people in concrete circumstances of a later time. When that sense meets with the sense of scripture—or lack of it—a face to face situation beyond both occurs. A sermon can be fashioned out of this meeting. Perhaps some example from the preacher's own life can be used as illustration. One story begets another.

But often the stories of this book admit of recasting in the preacher's own words. This will make a greater demand on the one who does it.

Even further, the stories can be read out as is, though they require a storyteller's self-surrender; he or she must become so deeply involved in what is told for eight or some minutes that he or she must seem to disappear. But on this level of presentation, the stories need a frame, some quick description of the scriptural readings the story relates to, then afterwards, some quick summation of the relationship between story and scripture. I include an example at the end of this Preface. Most often, though, people understand what has happened. Stories create active participants who see the story/scripture relationship for themselves.

Whatever way the stories are used, I intend them to show that the Sabbath is made for people, not people for the Sabbath. The issues in scripture are also found in people's lives. So a mutual interpretation can go on. If that is not so, liturgy—the Sabbath—and life develop separately, and liturgy becomes a haven from life, or life a haven from liturgy. These stories show that every moment of life is open to meaning, to a decision to make sense. Salvation and damnation are as secular as they are sacred. The stories are secular so we can think about people. Sacred language leaves little room for thinking, it is given, it is sanctioned, like the language in Butler's *Lives of the Saints*. St. Laurence on his griddle over the fire will always say, "Turn me over, I'm done on one side." An Iroquois warrior—witness Parkman's *The Jesuits in North America*—might break free, grab hot coals or burning logs and attack his captors, not to escape, but to defy their torture and thereby defeat them. Secular language shows God at work and the outcome uncertain because humans are involved, and their great freedom before God. And God becomes someone, something else than God, becomes whatever can touch the heart and turn it toward sense, away from nonsense. So human being develops. And scripture does also.

People listening to "Sabbath" stories such as those that follow can feel a personal input into scripture, they can feel how communities created scripture, how communities must keep creating it. E.g., "The Book of Jonah" was made up to correct the vengefulness of those who used savage psalms like #137 in the aftermath of the Babylonian captivity. The input is not a forgetting of the creaturely role. It is the remembrance of what love does when it is evoked, it procreates in some way. Also, the effect of these stories on people is that they feel they have entered liturgy as co-creators. Whether they agree with the sense of the stories or not. Maybe more so when they disagree. Their experience has been engaged and they respond to the whole liturgy with that experience once it is evoked. Then they start watching life outside liturgy in order to see God at work within the freedom of lives, or values at work which are sacred in some way. People remember stories and their meanings, the way the ancient monks remembered scriptural texts because of the beautiful chant set to them.

There are stories in this collection I would not use in church. The language in them is too realistic. That language is true to the stories and suits a public reading, but in a church setting it comes into conflict with the set-apart language that has developed in English since the change from Latin. That set-apart language, however, can express some very brutal things like revenge, conquest, hatred, killing—I've noted one psalm, but look also at psalms 18 and 109. So my decision not to use some stories in a sermon is political. I do, however, use the meanings I discovered through the writing of them.

For that is the main purpose of story, the discovery of meaning. Stories come out their own way, not the way the writer wants. They are not propaganda. Creating or hearing stories breeds an incarnational sense. Yes, one can abstract a message, but the message is like a soul yearning for a body and will not be whole without it. The wholeness teaches incarnation. To preserve a meaning, one has to maintain a wholeness. Then to preserve a person, one has to do the same. To preserve a history is to preserve a person, and his/her setting, his/her qualities. And the whole person is at stake in a happening or a choice or a behavior. We judge persons by categories now, and a category is a reduction to some one value, male, female, pro-life, pro-choice, terrorist, anti-terrorist, pro-nuke, anti-nuke. So we end up with "goods" and "bads," not with humans who are mixtures of a fearful and fascinating kind whom we had better know if there is to be salvation or damnation, not a predestination that voids us of sense.

Sermon Example
Body and Blood of Christ. (C)
Gen 14:18-20; 1 Cor 11:23-26; Lk 9:11b-17

The taste of bread and wine is a good taste. The taste of body and blood is sweet, the milk of a mother. It is hard to think that something good and sweet is a symbol of death. Unless that death gives life. It certainly did in the case of Jesus. He was an important man who preached the love of God. He could not be tormented out of the truth. He blessed creation at the end, He did not curse it. And we can live off everything He said and did. We can feel the life-giving nature of Him. We know it is the life of God, the life of God in someone's body and blood, translated into bread and wine, so everyone can eat.

We don't know Jesus dead, we know Him living. He has absorbed death. Death is written all over Him when He appears to His disciples. He has to remove from their minds the classical conviction that once dead, never alive again. Except perhaps as a memory. But Jesus is so physical to His disciples in apparitions to them! That is why they were so physical when they remembered Him. They took the same bread He did, the same wine He did, they meant what He meant. We can live off His innocence, we can live off His love, we can live off His blessing of the earth and all creatures in it. Such living may cost us our lives, as it cost Him His. But due to Him, death does not have the final say.

There is no doubt that people the world over want death to be a birth. We find shells in ancient graves, we find figurines of fertile women, we find symbols of the moon. It is as if people were asking womanhood for one more, for one greater procreation, to take in death and give out life. And to come out of that experience rich with nourishment. It may be hard for us to think of Jesus as womanly, but that is what He is in Eucharist. A modern parable may illustrate this.

There was a man who loved people's stories. He was a food salesman—to institutions, hospitals, nursing homes, and the like. He felt obliged to eat in the places where the food he sold was served, the breakfasts, the lunches, the dinners, and he would sit with people, staff and patients, and just pretend to be there for a vague reason. But he would get listening to a story and forget to ask how they liked the food. The nursery homes were the most poignant. One in particular. A woman there thought he was her son John. As soon as he entered the lobby where everyone was sitting she would shout, "O, there he is, there is John, my son," and she would come alive with joy. As he got close to her, however, she saw he wasn't, and she would get very sad and retreat back inside herself. But he would crouch by her wheelchair and bring her back out enough so she could tell him John was to come soon. Then there'd be some hope and expectancy in her. One day over lunch with the staff, a lunch steamed to death he thought, he asked about the woman. She had a son, it was true, but he had been killed in World War II, a hero, but a crazy man from what the staff could tell, he got a super medal from leading a suicide charge to gain the top of a hill and the battle. He had succeeded but he had also died. She had been in and out of institutions since that time, but now that she was old she was peaceful so she could live easily with the others. "Not much to live on," the man thought, "a dream of a son." One day he tried saying to her, "John was a hero, wasn't he?" She seemed for a moment to reflect on something, then she said, as if not to him, "He loved to kill things. I have to teach him not to. That is why he doesn't come to see me." Then the man tried something further, "John died in action, didn't he?" "O, yes," she said, "but he still wants to kill things. I have to teach him not to. I must soon or no one will."

"Why?" the man asked. "Why soon?" She lifted her head at him, almost fiercely, and whispered, "Well look at me!" Then she closed down on her self and drifted into sleep. And he did look at her. And he felt the power of womanhood as he had never felt it in his life. This woman would chase death to make it change its ways. "Crazy," he thought. "I just chase bad cooks. So they don't steam the red out of the carrots." He stood up and touched the woman on the forehead and said, "I hope you find him." Then he left.

The story of the man changes into the story of the woman then back into the story of the man. And that is the way the Eucharist moves, from Jesus, to us, then back to Jesus. And the great purpose of His, to chase death down and make it yield life, becomes our purpose. There was an ancient way of praying to Jesus, my brother, my sister, my mother, my father, my all. There was so much love in Him it called on every love.

Francis Patrick Sullivan, S.J.
(Sermon reprinted with permission from *Homilies For The Christian People*, ed. Gail Ramshaw, Pueblo Publishing Co., New York, 1989)

Double Bastard

*. . . the witness to Christ has indeed
been strong among you so that you will
not be without any of the gifts of the
Spirit while you are waiting for Our
Lord Jesus Christ to be revealed;*
—1 Corinthians 1:7

A priest got a letter from a music school asking if he had any old Roman hymn books with music and texts, the kind used by monastic and church choirs in the days of the Latin liturgy. If he did, would he sell the school some for courses they were offering in Gregorian chant. "I'll look," the priest thought. He was pastor of an old downtown church that once had a fine choir before families moved to richer places. The church was close to being shut by the diocese, it was that much on the edge financially. All the pastor's time seemed to be spent sweeping flecks of the ceiling from the floor and scrounging for money. This was a one man operation for the few elderly who came to the cavernous upstairs church for Mass. Not upstairs in winter though, it was heated only enough to keep the pipes from bursting. Mass was then downstairs. There was a hospital nearby, for which he was chaplain, and that job justified his life, which didn't have much left to it, ten years more in harness maybe, then out to stud as third assistant in the woods where the families had gone from this downtown parish.

So the priest went looking for the hymn books. In the downstairs sacristy. At one time, up and downstairs had been filled on Sunday. The choir had used the lower church organ for its practice sessions. The organist had been the director, and had, for years after the choir ceased, done all the weddings and funerals by himself, in the two churches up and down. Most of their contact had been the priest's intoning certain parts of the

1

Mass and the organist responding, two voices from opposite ends of the church who rarely met in the middle. There was not one Latin hymn book to be found in any of the closets. There were cassocks and surplices and piles of sheet music and stands for instrumentalists, plus some old tambourines for God knows what. There were even some banners for hanging over the choir loft railing on feast days. So the priest came back to the organ to see if a book might have been left in the organ bench. He lifted the bench lid and saw instead that it was filled with money, tens, twenties, fifties, and there were checks for similar amounts, but mostly slit envelopes with money in bill form spilling out.

"This organ hasn't been used since he died," the priest thought as he lowered the bench lid. He went quickly to the stairwell that led up to the rear of the main church, then to the stairwell that led up to the choir loft, went to the organ, lifted the lid of the bench and saw the same thing, it was filled with slit envelopes themselves filled with money. And the same scattering of checks. The priest returned to the rectory. He took several bank bags with him back into the church and filled them with what he found in the two organ benches. He noticed a certain fever in himself as he did so. "It's not the church's, not mine, it's the man's," he thought, "but nobody came to his funeral." He set four bags full on top of the organ console and looked up along the hollow church to the empty tabernacle, then at the flaking ceiling, then at the bare benches down below. He picked up each bag and threw it down from the loft onto the center aisle. "Bad money after bad!" he muttered.

He leaned against the console to calm himself. He could feel the oak of it and see the beautiful roll top cover for the banks of keys. He looked up at the pipes, some of them now tilting. He knew it was a great instrument. It would cost a fortune to repair. He went to a small door that led into the pipe area, opened it, and saw on the floor inside several stacks of just the book he was looking for. Must have been fifty of them. And he saw also the briefcase the organist had used, it was always bursting its clasp with sheet music. The priest released the clasp and opened the top. It was stuffed with money, and stuffed is the word, not packets, lettuce-like, fifties, hundreds, twenties, put there in haste. The priest stood up and nearly hit his head on the air chest. He looked up and saw that the mouths of the pipes above it were stuffed with money also, a whole bank of them. He looked down at the stacks of books and now noticed they were out of shape. So he lifted one and held it by the covers, inverted it and shook it and money drifted out and down to his feet. "That man is cursing me or blessing me," the priest thought. "He's got me on a trail to either one. I don't dare open the organ. But I'd better." He knew the key was on a nail just at the door into the pipe area, so he took it, opened the roll top, and as he started to push it upwards there was a cascade of bills that came out as if gravel out of a dump truck. They were all dollar bills. And inside, once the priest had the cover up, there were silver dollars on each of the banks of keys. "It'll be the same downstairs," the priest thought. "He did this the last week. He could hardly walk. But he knew we'd use the electronic up in the sanctuary for his funeral." The priest waited. "Tell me, you crazy bastard," he said low aloud, "you must have loved music! You couldn't have loved money!"

So the priest went down to the lower church and its organ. Sure enough, when he opened the roll top of the smaller instrument, a cascade of money came out. He left it there and went back to the sacristy closet where the old cassocks and surplices were hung packed together. As he separated them, sliding the hangers along the bar, money fell to the floor from between them. "Tell me, tell me!" the priest muttered again. "Music or money?" He walked back out of the closet and into the lower church. "It was money, wasn't it? You couldn't spend it. You want me to. You want me to save you." The priest stopped. Another feeling surged in him. "You double bastard! You want to see if I love it too!" He started again toward the choir section in back. "No! You didn't care about it. You're telling me the music died! And money won't make it live! Ahhh!" The priest sat in one of the empty pews. "You lived on love," he said. "You had a long slow death from it." Then after a minute. "You're right." Then another minute. "It's the same disease. I have it. But for a place. And there's no cure. Nobody knows. Until you're dead. And they clean up."

Along Came a Spider

'Console my people, console them,'
says your God,
'Speak to the heart . . .'
—Isaiah 40:1-2

"Some illusions maybe are good," a woman said. "They work for you."
The man she said it to was a bit drunk. He pushed his glass away. His
eyes came into focus. "See," he said, "perfectly sober." There was a
minute. Then his face collapsed like the wall of a glacier.

"Well, you produced a lot while she stayed with you," the woman continued. "You wrote better, you taught better, you even hit the golf ball
straight." "I should have stayed with you while I had the chance," the man
said. "I'm going to be celibate. See if I can't be a spider." "Some illusions
are bad," the woman said, "they work against you."

He started to reach for the glass. Then stopped. "I was celibate before,
you know that. Tibet is Chinese now or I'd go back to being like a prayer
wheel." "Bad," she said. "But it has tremendous stability," he said, "the
soul gets so peaceful. Nothing can harm it." "You came home a bag of
bones," she said, "chicken soup for a month. Your soul was evaporating."
"I guess some people can sustain it," he said. "I can't sustain anything.
Not finally. Some quality disappears. I didn't love her after all, it's why
she went, I'm sure."

"You were always like frostbite to me," the woman said, "but I knew
that early. So you really never had a chance to stay."

"Frostbite," he said. She said nothing more.

"I'm that to myself," he said, "maybe not bite, but frost for sure. I
remember when I was a little kid, an old couple down the street committed

4

suicide. They took a funnel, attached a rubber hose to it, turned on the stove gas and inhaled through the funnel. Somebody smelled the gas, broke the windows, then went in when the gas cleared, but it was too late. I remember seeing the funnel and tube in the ashcan. I felt that the instrument of death should somehow be saved and put in a sacred place, in a church, and have a red vigil light near it, a prayer that wouldn't go out." He stopped and took the drink in his hand. "This is like one of the holders. Stubby candle inside. They last eight hours." He stopped again, then slowly tipped the drink out on the tablecloth where it was soaked up.

"So okay," the woman said, "I've sat here for an hour and commiserated with you. My duty's done and I'm bored stiff." "Well," the man said, looking a little more alive, "that's a good sting. Like peroxide. Cold and cleansing." "Give up the illusion," she said to him, "that one anyway. No woman is going to do it for you, you're permafrost. And no God is going to do it for you either, unless it's one of those deities of the void." "Tell me the secret?" he asked. "I don't have one," she said. Then she stopped. "Except maybe how I dress in the morning. I put on clothes I want the day to be." "Women are my clothes," he said. She laughed, said nothing. "They're nice when they fit," he went on. "They never fit," she said. "So clothes are not it," he said. She knew he was asking for a real answer.

"What have I got to do with you?" she asked, a little angry now that her gesture of charity was over, and the dinner was over, and so was this strange date with an ex-husband whose second woman had left him. "I thought you were a friend," he said. "I am not anything to you," she said, "not anything you have a hold on." "Okay," he said, "that's as good an answer as any man can get. Or any woman." "What do you mean by that?" she asked. "You said some illusions are bad," he answered. "Mine of you as a friend, for example. I'm sort of watching dominoes fall. What'll I be when they're all down?" "You'll be like me," she said. "You'll choose what you put on. You'll choose what you take off. They will only be clothes."

"But I was like that once," he answered, "don't you remember? I met you and it was like waking up from the dead. Are you suggesting that I go back there?" "Really," she said, "what are you asking me?" "Why aren't you dead inside? What is the secret? You have no one. You don't seem to want anyone. You're not troubled." She looked at him, emotions calm again, and said, "I am not dead inside because now I want the truth, I don't care what it costs me. And if the truth is someone doesn't love me, I live with that. And if the truth is someone loves me but badly, I live with that too. I know what I love. And I know why. It is not myself." She waited for a few moments. "You didn't love a thing when you came home," she continued, then caught herself and the rising tone of her voice. She went on more calmly, "But when she came along, I thought you did love her, and I thought that was good." "But it wasn't," he broke in, "I do not love." "You don't have to," she said, "there are things you can do that have marvelous effects to them. They are no consolation. But they do not create frostbite." "Tell me how you know this," he asked. She spread her hands palm up on the table as if to say, "Look at me after you!" He understood. He could not ask the next question. So she answered it, but indirectly. "When I dress in the morning, I often choose fabric over color. And I behave like that fabric during the day. I mean behave toward other people. And toward myself. You will end up loving."

The answer stripped him as bare as anything she had ever seen. He had nothing left but choice. And she saw the choice. And how it took him over. Then he said, "I remember that a family came to live in that house where the old people had taken the gas pipe. It was a family that never took a bath. When we played pickup football we never wanted to tackle either of the two older boys, they smelled that badly. There was a girl and another boy. I saw the boy get hit by a truck. They were sledding down an icy hill right angles to a street and a van couldn't stop. And the van driver was an ex-con. The scene stopped there. I don't remember what I did. But you know, the scene just started again."

She reached for her purse on the floor beside her chair. Her cheeks had flushed. He knew she saw what he saw. "Can I pay for us both?" he asked. "Yes," she said. "I'll be back in a minute."

Fishy Thing

*. . . think before you do anything—hold
on to what is good, and avoid every form
of evil.*
—1 Thessalonians 5:21

A man was happy with wintertime. Before the snow came. When frost
touched things, trees, bushes, sidewalks. There was clarity, visibility, and
nothing was being killed. He knew too much about killing. Down on the
docks where he worked. The last one he had seen was the day before, out
the office window. There was a phone booth at the gate. A man in it, door
closed. A woman came along the sidewalk, bandanna over her head, fur
collar up against the cold. She stopped outside the booth and the man inside sensed something and turned. He saw a woman so he relaxed some
and kept talking. The woman kicked the door on its central hinge. It
slammed open. Then she emptied a police 38 into the man inside. Then
she turned and ran shoeless out of sight back the way she had come.

The man watching from the window knew it was not a woman. He
recognised the face under the bandanna. He backed away from the window. No one in the office with him. He saw nothing. And when the police
showed and went asking all over the place who saw what, he gave his con-
vincing shrug of the shoulders and pointed to the ship manifests he was
checking on the computer when he heard the backfires, motorcycle he
thought. "Sorry. Like to help you out," he had said.

As he walked now through the woods he realized how many killings he
had seen just by sheer chance, and no one knew until now or he'd have
been dead long ago. The woman who had done the killing was the
toughest longshoreman he had ever met, and the smartest. He was so set
on getting those who had killed his wife and kid with dynamite in the car

that he was into disguises. Unlike him. In the old days, he'd have walked into hell with his name flashing like a Goodyear blimp at night. Now, he had to catch people unawares. He did it from a wheelchair one day. In a hospital where one of his enemies was under care for frostbite, from hiding in a warehouse where he had gotten drunk and the watchman who found him had the police haul him to city hospital. The wheelchair had a man wearing a bathrobe in it. He had a bandage around his head and a towel folded across his lap. In the towel, a gun, which he emptied into the frostbitten guy seated between the beds in a two bed room. The killer then ran out a fire exit, jumped back in his clothes and vanished into the freezing night. Somebody had told him where his victim was. There was another day he did it as a drunken bum collapsed in a doorway with a stream of urine out from him and freezing on the sidewalk. Near a café his enemies thought safe. He hit a guy and his woman with two shotgun blasts. The man walking through the woods could remember that one as vividly as any. He'd been told the hospital story, but had see the bum one from his car as he was driving from late breakfast back to the dock where another ship was starting at noon.

But the killing up on the crane had been the worst. The killer simply climbed the rung ladder underneath the cab. The operator sensed nothing and kept lifting the container and was swinging it from the dock aboard ship with everyone watching stock still until they sensed that the container might drop on them. That's when they ran and the operator noticed. He halted the thing in mid air, threw open the cab door and looked down, which he should never have done. He got it right in the head and fell by the gunman onto the footing of the crane way below. The killer climbed down rung by rung and disappeared. He was dressed like a customs officer.

The fishy thing about it all was that the killer was being fed info by the law as well as by the lawless. And the man walking in the woods knew the principle that was in operation: "Let them kill each other. They're all guilty, but nobody could ever prove it in court." The man walking through the woods agreed with that principle. So far very few innocents had been harmed. And he had innocents at home. A woman and three kids. But they might not remain innocents long. The police were being forced to end the slayings. They had set him up, had said to the killer that he was ready to finger him. And they had said to the killer's enemies where the killer was likely to be the following morning. So tomorrow when the man walking in the woods showed up for work, he knew that the killer and the enemies would be there. The police had told him, but indirectly, so they could deny it, he'd never know how they placed him at those scenes of crime. The killer would get him first. The enemies would get the killer, and the police would gun down whoever was left standing. The man's breath congealed in the air in front of him, then disappeared into the frosty scene. "So I go to work," he thought. "The principle is right, let them kill each other. He'll come maybe as a woman again. French Canadian trucker. No speak the English. Have trouble parking the trailer so he can look around. They'll come in taxis to pick up stuff from Customs. A few at a time. Go in next door to me and be friends. Wait for him to come after me. In his stuffed jeans and stuffed lumberjacket and wig and sunglasses. So I put a sign on my door: DOUBLE CHECK WITH CUSTOMS. Maybe he'll figure it out. They won't. They want him so bad."

The man stopped and looked around at the new growth birches and the older hemlocks. The woods behind his house went for miles this way. Then he thought, "Customs people will get killed if he goes in there first." He started walking again. "So who do I save?" he asked himself. "He won't kill family. They will if they live. Mine. And they won't kill Customs. Too hot. But he will. And I'm gone either way. Only ones free are the cops. Unless they're stupid and jump in too soon." He turned back toward his house, crossed a plank over the small creek and picked up the woods road between some crumbling stone walls. The road crossed an old railroad line. The sign was still there on its pole and fastened by rusty screws. A big X with the words STOP LOOK LISTEN just legible between the arms of the X. "He'll get this," the man said, as he banged the sign free with a rock. "And get me. But he'll be ready when they come in."

As he walked down the street toward his house, he thought, "Customs will be safe." Then, "The principle is right."

4th Sunday, Advent

Bye Bye Wrinkles

*The angel Gabriel was sent by God to a
town in Galilee called Nazareth, to a
virgin betrothed to a man named Joseph,
of the House of David; and the virgin's
name was Mary.*
—Luke 1:26

A woman taught bible school to children after church during their school year. She had done so for a long time thinking that as the twig is bent so the tree is inclined. She had not married. Her fiancé had been killed in the Korean War. She worked for the State Department, an analyst for Middle Eastern Affairs, so she had drowned her grief in that endless morass of problem. The grief had turned into absorption. But she broke the spell every Sunday with eight year olds. You had to tell them stories, not dogmas. So here it was, Advent season, and she had to deal with skies that opened and hearts that closed and comings and goings between the heavens and the earth. She noticed two things this year. They, the children, didn't believe a word she said, the stories were boring. And she was teaching them beauty, not God. Or she was trying to.

One Sunday she had taken them and a few willing parents to the National Gallery where they had seen madonnas, early ones from the Byzantine Period, later ones from the Renaissance. And she had pointed out one superb Fra Angelico, the Annunciation. "Look how lovely the gold lacing is on the angel's wings!" she had said. "And the body is so light it seems to have no weight, but the lines make it part of our world, and so do the colors." Then she had spoken of the Virgin, how like the Angel she was, except she seemed to have weight, but it was the weight of cloth, dyed silk, "Like this scarf I'm wearing," she said. And she handed the scarf around.

10

The children began to toss it a bit, treating it as a balloon, and one of the taller girls floated it over the teacher's head so it drifted down on her and she looked like someone from another painting. They were enjoying her more than Fra Angelico. "But look at the Virgin's beautiful cheeks!" she said to the group before they left. Some of the boys groaned. They wanted sandpaper. One of them leaned against her and said, "They're frozen stiff." "God doesn't want them to move," a girl said.

"She'll never grow old," a third voice said. It was an old voice, a visitor who had come up behind the group, a woman quite elderly, quite wrinkled, but quite vigorous. "Look at me!" she said to the group. And they did turn. "Want me to fly around on my cane?" she said. She had one, and started to put it between her legs. The children giggled and moved around her. And the woman pointed to the Fra Angelico and the Virgin on it and said again, "She'll never grow old. But something else is in that picture. Now what? Tell me! Look at it and look at me and tell me?" "You used to look like that," one boy said. "You moved," another boy said, "and you got wrinkled." The old woman laughed. "So anybody who moves gets wrinkled. How come you're all so smooth?" She touched a few faces. "You get it back," a girl said. "Just girls," a boy said, "we don't want it back." "Laser beams," a second boy said, "pow!" "Okay," the old woman said, "laser beams. But they burn their food then can't eat it." The group groaned Yuck! and began to move away for something new.

"Go out in the rotunda and watch the waterfall," the bible teacher said, "be out in a minute." Then she turned to the old woman and said, "You should have flown." "The kids are right, though," the old woman said, "Fra Angelico froze everything in beauty. The Virgin didn't look like that next to the Cross. And I bet she was worn when she died." "I bet she wanted to be," the bible teacher said. "She probably didn't even think of it," the old woman said, "nobody in the Middle East looks like much after a few years. Vanity's not a problem. Maybe the only one they don't have after the age of thirty." The bible teacher laughed. "The rest of the problems are my field," she said. "Bible's kind of a weekend relief. And the art that goes with it."

"You don't believe a word," the old woman said. The bible teacher was silent. "What screwed things up?" she then said as a kind of reply. "I did," the old woman said, "I told the angel to leave. And not ever to come back." The bible teacher looked at her and said, "Until the wrinkles came." "Yes," said the old woman, "but I don't miss the skin, believe me, it's the voice, it's the voice that goes with someone wanting you and you wanting someone back." "The angel doesn't want you anymore," the bible teacher said, "nice angel!" "Oh, there's one that wants me," the old woman replied, "but he's a rubbish collector and all apologies." The two women looked at the picture. "So we don't get a second chance?" the bible teacher asked. "I keep listening," the old woman said, "and keep wondering if I have anything to give." "You want to give?" the bible teacher asked. "Yes," the old woman said, then said it again, "yes, and not rubbish! But it's all I have! He had more, Fra Angelico, but it's rubbish too, lovely, lovely!" "What wouldn't be?" the bible teacher added. "She's the only purity, there, in paint, on a wall, but with a humidifier next to her, so she doesn't flake." "I would die for this painting," the older woman said, "and everything in it." She paused. "And for them too!" She pointed her cane through the door towards the rotunda where the children and the few adults were waiting. "But no one would ever ask me." "Good thing," said the bible teacher. "Not a good thing," said the old woman, "not a good thing when you think about it. There'd be no angel. And no Virgin." "Funny, you're right," the bible teacher said, "scares you, doesn't it!" "Yes," said the old woman, "right out of your skin." And she put a hand on the bible teacher's arm and started to laugh softly. "Not bad, eh!" she said at her own pun. Then, "You go or you'll lose your flock. A shepherd without sheep is worse." "Bye," said the bible teacher. "Bye," said the old woman.

Midnight Mass, Christmas

Up by the Roots

Caesar Augustus issued a decree for a census
of the whole world to be taken . . . and
everyone went to their own town to be
registered.
                                    —Luke 2:1,3

A man was in Jerusalem for Christmas. His mother was buried there, in
a convent cemetary. After she was a widow and he and his brother were
grown, she came and joined a group of nuns who worked for religious
unity. They ran a hostel and conferences and did refugee work. He rarely
saw her during the twenty years she had spent doing it. He was estab-
lishing his own family and career. That was now done, but it was not
enough. So the last five years he left home at Christmas and came to
Jerusalem. He was back by the feast of Epiphany and that was the day of
gift giving. His wife and children saw his trip as an imitation of the Gospel
story, the head of the household going to check in at a place sacred to them
all. They knew that when they could they would go with him, in a few
years time, when the children were all mid-teens and self-propelled.

Jerusalem was sacred to the man because of his mother. She had always given of herself to the point of frenzy. He had run away from home
twice when he was young just to avoid her generosity. He hid out the
second of those times in a windowless warehouse, as unyielding looking a
place as you could ever find, a blank facade with steel doors. But cold and
hunger brought him home. And strange thing, she had done nothing when
he walked in the door, twelve years old and beaten by his own rebellion.
She had just stood there motionless, like a mannequin, though her cheeks
flushed deeper and deeper with the struggle for self control. Then she
started to move like a robot, robot motions putting on a kettle to heat

13

water, robot motions opening a tin of hot chocolate, robot motions setting the table and putting cold cuts and bread on it because hunger needed quick relief. But she began to weep during this machine-like service and so did he, so while she sat stiffly in one chair with the tears running down her cheeks, he sat in the other eating a sandwich soggy from the tears pouring down his. After his stomach had stopped roaring, he had gotten up and gone behind her straight back, reached between her shoulder blades and turned off an imaginary button. Then he put his arms around her from behind and held her as if she were the child and he the parent. His father came home later exhausted from looking. He was a man of great faith in her so when she signalled him to ask nothing, that something had been healed, he kept silence and sat to a meal she had prepared for him.

From that day on the son noticed his mother looking out into the larger world for room to show her generosity. And their friendship deepened. He always had to ask before she would do anything for him, and he always did, but only for what he really needed, which was mostly encouragement, and encouragement he got with an intensity that left him exhilarated. But she never took his freedom away again. So now he was running towards her, not away, and she had been dead five years. Each time he went to the grave he recovered an exhilaration that kept him going a long time after.

"Well, I finally got her into the ground," he heard a man's voice say to him in a prize-winning New York accent. "thoid time never fails." They were both on the parapet of the King David Hotel looking at the Jaffa Gate into Jerusalem not a quarter of a mile away, and inside that gate, King David's Tower. "Who?" the man asked. He loved New York accents. "Mother," was the answer. "You been trying?" the man asked. "Foist time we come she promises me," the New Yorker answered, "says go home I'm incurable. But her Doctor phones from the States and says he's got a new pill. So we pile in the plane, go home, the pill don't work, we pile in the plane again and come back here. She wants to be buried over on Mount Olivet there. You a Christian? You know about it then. I'm Jewish. When the Messiah comes, the people buried there get up foist and go dancing in the streets." "So what happened?" the man asked. The New Yorker answered, "She got scared. It's all rock over there. She likes green things growing. She has my father's grave back home looking like a jungle. Take me back, put me beside your father, she says. So back we go and we remember she hated my father. 'I want to die in Jerusalem,' she says again. 'The Messiah is a good guy, not a bum.' So we come back. And my business is going down the chute. And you know what happened back here?" "No," the man said, "what?" "She sneaks away from me," the New Yorker answered, "takes a cab to a travel agent to get a ticket home, doesn't wear warm clothes, catches pneumonia, nothing we can do to stop it, and dies down in the Hadassah Hospital telling me she gotta get back to New York." "You put her on Mount Olivet?" the man asked. "Yeah," the New Yorker said and his voice thickened. He started to cry, facing out toward the city, hoping the other man would protect him a bit from being seen. "Like somebody pulled you up by the roots," the New Yorker continued. "Never felt this before. Something's crying inside me."

"My mother's buried in a convent, there to the north, near the Damascus Gate," the man said. "You know what I mean then," the New Yorker said. "One more time back and forth," he went on, "and *I'd* be the stiff in the ground. Good place for her though. Messiah's a tough guy. Have to be to handle her." And he started to cry again. "Look, friend," said the first man, "we're standing inside what they gave us, these bodies. Let's make believe we're both messiahs and go have a drink. And make believe we can deal with any woman on the face of the earth."

"Yeah," the New Yorker said, "yeah," and he turned and he buried his face in the first man's chest and shook for a while, holding the man's arms. Then he backed off and said, "I hope the real messiah comes. Or she'll get up and use that ticket she bought." "Quick, cancel it," the first man said. And he took the New Yorker by the arm and steered him toward the lobby. "Too late," the New Yorker said, "I put it in the coffin just in case." And they both laughed like fools all the way to the lounge.

Tricks of the Trade

It was for no reason except
compassion that God saved us!
Titus 3:5

A woman ran a fruit and vegetable store. It was her father's. But he was in a home and drifting off. So it was her store, one she had grown up in. She was not much for school, but had learned a great deal from people and produce. Forget her marriage, it had been five years of mistake, made for her father so he could have a son around, an immigrant son who was happy until he mastered English and then some tricks of the trade. He was getting rich on those tricks somewhere else, with someone else. Neat divorce and no claims. And no children. Just fruit and vegetables for discriminating customers in a neat suburb. It was like selling reproductions of art. She had to judge color and shape and texture and heft. She had to match what she judged with some qualities in customers.

Recently she had added select cheeses to her stock. The fruit/cheese combo was old world and attractive. In fact, she had a stand up table, small, circular, where she put samples along with some no name red and white wines, bits of fruit, bits of cheese, small plastic glasses. Someone suggested she put coffee there too, so she did, a pot of Colombian with demitasse cups and a bowl of cane sugar. Someone suggested beet sugar, so she put another bowl there and labeled it. People ended up staying in the store for longer periods and talking, to her, to one another, but that didn't cut into the service. She kept her help on their toes, not by command, but by extra pay depending on how business went. And she never had to face robbers. Nor raises in rent. Her father owned the business block. So she did. A perfect life.

16

Until the day a robber did come in. Neatly dressed. In an overcoat and hat with cleaned shoes. He handed her a shopping list of groceries which fooled her for a second as she read down through the carrots, beans, kiwi fruit, to the postscript: "All your money in the bottom of the bag or I take out my gun and ruin peoples' day. Look inside my coat." She looked up. His coat was now partly open, she could see the butt of a gun just above his belt. He closed the coat and buttoned it. "Sure," she said. She took a large brown bag, filled the order, went to the register, rang up the sale, then deftly took all the bills out of the drawer and put them down inside the larger bag that held the smaller ones, then said, "Your change." He saw she was absolutely free of the money, that she had memorized his face, and was really saying, "You may not even be worth turning in for five hundred bucks."

"I forgot parsley," he said. "Parsley's no good yet," she said, "I wouldn't sell it." "What else have you got?" he asked. He was not touching the bag with the produce and the money. "Customers," she said, "who, in another minute, are going to sense something. So take this bag and go. Or leave it and go." "How do I go?" he asked. "This way," she said, and she walked from behind the small counter, put her arm through his and turned him toward the door and began to walk with him as if with an old friend. "I'll send the bag out at eleven," she said, loudly enough to make the scene look right. "We used to go out at eleven," he said, "after the mist lifted. So you could see. See jungle, though. Not them. They could see you and take you out before you could drop. Are you taking me out?"

They were at the door. She kept her arm in his. Her help were at the cash register and saw it was empty. They had nothing to make change with. She opened the door and went out on the sidewalk with the man. "There's nothing in front of me," he said. "The litter can," she said, "where you can drop the gun. It'll go with the litter." She moved him towards it. His hands did nothing. So she freed his coat and took the gun by the butt and dropped it in the can. It was very light. Traffic was busy. People wouldn't notice. "Where will I send the groceries?" she asked. She noticed that her help were standing at the door, though they hadn't seen the gun maneuver, and that people inside were at the window with very courious looks on their faces. "I have nothing behind me," he said. "Fire can come in from any side. I can't get low enough. From the trees. I'm afraid to look. They see you look."

She heard a small screech of tires behind her on the street outside the cars parked at the curb. A door opened. She saw a woman of about sixty get out, her face flooded with fear, and she came toward the two standing by the litter can as someone comes toward bad news. "Did he do anything?" the older woman asked. "He can't do anything," the store woman said. "Not until I'm sure," the man said, "I can't wave anyone on until I'm sure. They let the point man pass." "He's gentle," the older woman said, "but I'm always afraid. And I have to keep him. Until I can't. He disappeared on me today." "He had a gun," the store woman said. "A plastic toy," the older woman said. "But you could charge him." "Somebody else might," the store woman said, "take him." The older woman did.

People back in the store saw some sense in what was happening, someone not all there being handled like a child by two women. The older woman took the man by the arm and led him towards the car. But he turned and said, "When the mist clears you see the flowers too. But you have to know you can't. They were behind the flowers. The flowers took us out." "Not here," the store woman said, "here people shoot flowers." The man seemed to come to, as if out of a waking dream. He shrugged off his mother's hand and looked around in some panic. "It's okay," she said, "it's okay, there's no harm, I'll explain, please, just get in the car." They drove off.

The store woman went back inside. People were standing there waiting. "He was harmless," she said. "From Vietnam. He couldn't kill. So he broke. Like a dream. So please, some fruit, some cheese, some coffee. Normal." She took extra money out of her purse and put it in the register so the help could make change. For some reason she could not touch the bag of fruit and money. She left it standing on the small counter. As if waiting.

Christmas Mass, Christmas Day

Jeanie-in-the-Box

...from his fullness we have,
all of us, received—yes, grace in
return for grace.
—John 1:16

"You should shop all year for Christmas," a saleswoman once said to a man who was looking for things at the last minute. "Right," the man had answered as he chose things he knew wouldn't fit, but were expensive enough to soothe over the wrong sizes. Yet her advice had started him shopping all year. Then started him giving all year, why tuck things in the back of a closet where their value was in escrow. He looked for shells for his wife. Heavy metal rock for his daughter. Model trains for his son who owned the attic and moved freight from one end of it to the other. One could feel the house shake, one thought.

He rarely bought anything for himself. It was curious how little he needed, his family, his job as a researcher with the Encyclopedia Brittanica, his work for local government, volunteer stuff. "I'm a perfect square," he thought. "Maybe I should picket a war memorial or something, become gracefully notorious." But his unease was deeper than some graceful notoriety could cure. He was sensing that everything had a beautiful form, but that everything was away from that form as if in some exile. An example was his mother who was now old and fragile, though she insisted on living alone near his sister and her family. She had been extraordinarily beautiful, photographs showed it. His son looked like her, and his daughter was angry about not getting those good looks herself. She was stuck with his big nose which came with his father's side of the genes. She was talking plastic surgery at the tender age of fifteen. He kept telling her that punk rock would love her nose, but she heard that as the

19

20 All Eyes and Blind

sarcasm it was. He wouldn't change her. She had a passion that would roost well once this flapping was over. And he wasn't thinking chicken, he was thinking fish hawk, osprey, the kind that sit on pilings out in the bay and are masters of flight above and below water. He loved to watch them skim just a few feet above their own reflections and never notice. It's as if they pulled fish out of their own hearts.

The man's sense that everything had a form it was absent from began to torment him. Because he sensed too that he was as absent from himself as were the rest. That came out most often when he tried to buy a present for himself. He actually felt drawn to music boxes. Lift a lid and hear a charmer of a sound. The same everytime. He remembered the story of the emperor and the nightingale. How the emperor was afraid the beauty of the nightingale's song would vanish if the bird decided to leave. So the emperor had a mechanical songster made. But he missed the free gift. And the machine broke after constant playing. So the emperor was sad and sick in his old age. Until the living bird came and sang to him and made him well. Then the bird left and the emperor no longer wanted to cling to life and died happy without the bird.

"You're looking for a God," a pawnbroker said to him one day. Pawnshops were often the best places to find old music boxes. The owner had a smile on his old face as he said it. He was pure oriental in looks, but had a pure American accent that said origin San Francisco. They were opening the lids of various boxes he had on a back shelf. One had just played, "How many miles to London town." "Everything is right about these things except the songs," the man said, "you rarely get a good song." "Right," the owner said, "a minute or two of something, no jazz, no rock." They opened a Stephen Foster "*Jeanie With The Light Brown Hair.*" "Ever hear Marilyn Horne sing this?" the man asked. "Yup," said the owner, "once, on the radio, couldn't believe it, she should be Brunhilde with helmet and buckler bashing the gods with that larynx." "Is this lacquered wood?" the man asked. "Yup," said the owner, "but see, the wood is inlaid, and the color comes from the wood, not paint. I figure it was done with tweezers. And it's really wisteria, light purple wood, would you believe it?" "Goes with Jeanie's eyes, not her hair," the man said. "Goes with the mood of the song," the owner said, and he opened the lid again until they came to the lines "on the soft summer air." Then he closed it.

"I won't sell it to you, I'll give it to you." "I couldn't take it," the man said, "it's worth too much." "Not to anybody but you and me and the old lady who had it. She's gone." "Can't I buy something else?" the man asked. "Sure," the owner said, "how about a banjo for the kitchen with Dinah. Needs strings though. These'll snap. Or there's this four legged, two headed alarm clock. Give you bursitis winding it." They were both laughing. "I make my money on old gold," the owner said, "you'd be surprised. So take the box. It's not God but the next best thing." "Jeanie's the next best thing," the man said. The owner giggled, "You are right, but she goes in a different box." His voice went sad. The man lifted the music box lid, it had been placed in his hand. He let the song play to the end. He closed the lid and rubbed the wisteria pattern with his fingertips. "I have to give you something for this, it's too lovely." "You couldn't pay for it," the owner said, "it was *my* old lady's. I turn the others on sometimes. This has the best sound. The best of those you keep. The real best goes." "You should want to keep it," the man said.

"Oh, what's the matter with you," the owner said, "you don't know it's a music box? I thought you did. You do. But you are afraid." "I am afraid," the man said. "Of what?" the old man asked. "To be owned," the man said, and said it as an admission. "No one can own you," the old man responded, "you die too. Then someone loves you or you are nothing." "I'll take this," the man said. "Okay," the old man responded, "but here, wrap it in this chamois cloth and put it in your pocket so it doesn't look like a buy. Funny how heavy it is." "Where'd you get it, I mean she?" "From a customer one day. For a lot of money, I couldn't believe it. No one comes back for that, I said. And she said no one. She just loved it. So I never sold it. So you can't either. You have to give it. But wait for the right one." "Someone who loves it?" the man asked. "No, no," the old man said, "someone who loves Jeanie."

Holy Family Sunday

Woman Talk

. . . you can let your servant go in peace, just as you promised, because my eyes have seen the salvation which you have prepared for all the nations to see.

—Luke 2:29-31

A young woman was talking to her grandmother. They were great friends. "I don't want to marry," she said. "There's less of a lie when you get old." The grandmother said nothing. She just looked at her lovely young woman. Who said next, "They are squeezing you, aren't they? They want your money now." "Yes," said the grandmother, "and they'll think you're after some too." "So there's no love?" the granddaughter asked. "There's a little," the grandmother said, "and maybe a little is enough." "Grandmother, you're not buying that little, are you? That's as bad as what they're doing." "You're a rare creature, my dear," the grandmother said. "Every time you come through that door I sense how precious life has been and I'm glad of every second. If you could be bought I'd die." "Please don't dodge me," the young woman said. "I'm buying that little," the grandmother answered. There was a look of shame on her face. "Only with your grandfather did I feel it was free. And with you. He's been gone so long! And you've scarcely arrived. But what a pair you are, even to your eyes."

"Don't buy them, grandmother, tell them to live from their own strength." "I don't know if I could face being alone," the grandmother said, "and besides, the money is of no use to me." "Oh, that's an excuse," the young woman said, and she got up and walked around the room. "Not only do I not want to marry, I do not want to be old," she said. She stopped and

22

looked at her grandmother. "Can't you tell me something that will free me?" The grandmother was now visibly shaken. Because she knew what the question meant. "I will tell you that there is the way you intend things. And there is the way things come out. And I always intended things with love. And only sometimes did they come out with love. I do not know what I would do without love. And I have almost no claim on it left. Now wait and let me think."

She paused and it was a long while her granddaughter stood facing her. Then the grandmother said, "I think you should intend to love with every ounce of you. That stays with you. Even though it stays with me badly. Though I think today teaches me something. How much I love you! How much you let me! Maybe that's it, letting people have the chance, however few take it. I can't tell you how much I love!" She turned her head away a bit then back. "And I don't mean the past. I mean now, you, standing there in my husband's body, yes, just the way you stand. And I have this thirst to see your life. I don't know what it will be, and I would never tell you."

"Grandmother, they don't know this," the young woman said, "and I don't want to bring a brood like that into my life and get left in a chair with just a checkbook." "Well," the grandmother said, "do you see what can be touched in me that cannot yet be touched in you? You just see how things came out. Your father, your uncles, your aunts, your cousins. But I remember nights of conceiving. And I remember births, though the doctors used to knock me out. I resent that now. And I remember language. And I remember the beginnings of womanhood and manhood. What I can't remember is standing right here in front of me. I can't tell you how much more I want for you, more than that narrow womanhood I had. But not some busy, busy, and when you wake up you have a checkbook but no people. I mean no one like yourself to ask you for your soul."

The young woman let out a breath she had been holding. "I guess I did, ask you for your soul," she said, "maybe that's worse than asking for money." "It could be," the grandmother said, "it could be if my soul is too small and you have to live knowing that, that I'm some little creature you have to let go of, or treat like a child because God said you should be kind." The young woman smiled. "No, grandmother, size isn't it, I wanted to see if you had one at all, down below all the family talk. My father is like some pinball machine. And my mother is now like a pup that can't stop barking until you hit it on the nose. So I asked myself how far back this went. And how far forward. And do I want to stop this thing with me."

"Something like this happened to me, I think," the grandmother said. "I was your age. My mother and father were from Ireland, and a half of them was always back there, it was the time of the troubles and family were getting killed or were on the run and feared dead. But one cousin of my father's was captured and on a hunger strike in a jail someplace. And my father was caught up in the fervor of it because it was bringing shame on the jailers, on those who held the country against its will. My father was for the hunger strike even until death. And he said that at table one Sunday, there were four of us children, and my mother had just put a roast beef in front of us, and all the food was steaming there too, mashed potatoes, squash, lovely cauliflower with cream sauce, and green snappy beans. Well, she stood from her place and she picked up the roast beef on a plate and she hurled it back out through the door to the kitchen. 'Damn him and his stupid fast!' she said. Then she picked up each other dish and they followed flying through the kitchen door to smash against the corner of the cast iron stove. 'Damn their hatred of life! We didn't give them bodies for that!' She was raging to herself we knew, not against my father. He was really too good a man, though blind on this one thing. When she was through hurling she stood back hardly able to breathe and she had her hands over her belly where we all came from and she said his name the way his friends said it, 'Bat'—he was Bart to her, though she said Father mostly in front of us, as he said Mother, though she was Joan—'Bat, that fast is a curse on me and every woman! 'Ah!' he said, and after a minute to recover he went to her and they just leaned together and we were in some dream we couldn't understand. Then he said, 'Well, we can't feed them broken dishes.' So the two of them washed the roast beef off, and she made some gravy and we had delicious open-faced sandwiches. He never spoke of the fast again, though the cousin died. I think my father even became a pacifist." She paused a bit. "I come from her," she said then.

The granddaughter did not wait but said immediately, "You do. And I hope I do. And not from the cousin. But I'm afraid. And I'm afraid I'll breed cousins and not your mother." "You have no way of knowing," the grandmother said. "Yes I do," said the granddaughter. "Oh, you do have a way," said the grandmother, "no children. I don't know how you intend love by that unless you become a sister or someone charitable for a whole lifetime. There are so many ways now." "That's wise," the young woman said. Then the grandmother went on, "And do not fear old age. It's soon over." That caught the young woman. She flushed deeply. The grandmother saw it. "You are what she looked like that day," she said. "She couldn't hide a thing."

The Solemnity of Mary, Mother of God

Body Bags

"May the Lord uncover his face to you and bring you peace." This is how they are to call my name . . . and I will bless them.
—Numbers 6:26-7

"The olive trees mean war, not peace," a young man said. He was talking to his father. They were both looking across a small valley to a grove on the opposite hill. "They are our trees," the father said with fury, "you cannot leave until we have them again or are buried in this ground. I will curse you if you go." "You are a curse already," the son said. The father faced him livid and raised his stick. The son grabbed at the stick and caught it. The father tried to pull it away then strike. Both ended in a tug of war. The son was too strong.

"Then I double the curse," the father said. "You'd have to kill her again to double it," the son said. "What are you saying?" the father asked. "You were not working that day," the son said, "you were behind a wall when she confronted that crowd. That crowd was killing an innocent woman. And you knew it too. My mother and that woman talked the whole night. That woman had not spent the night in the field with an enemy. She had spent the night on the roof above you talking. And the two of them were hit with the same stones. It should have been you first!" "You are a woman," the father hissed. "Yes," the son said, "I am from her." "Then you are nothing," the father said. And he turned and slammed the now free stick down on a wooden table, bouncing dirt up out of its cracks. Then he threw it over a low brick wall down into the scrub where he startled a few goats who skipped a bit then resumed eating. "From her, I am everything you are not," the son said. "She was the real olive grove. You had her in your possession. But she was peace. And you needed war as those goats need thistles." "You are like bad water, you kill the ground," the father said. "Now go! And take another name. I remove your name!"

"It is just as well," the son said, "the enemy will not make the same mistake twice." The father suddenly became very wary. He knew there were more words coming. "Yes, a new officer, with an old list, and a message to me," the son continued, "for further information about who had come in as someone's relative, and was the new leader, a message with my pay check. And I saw how you answered when you signed your own check. And I even know which teller you went to in the bank. You always went to the same one. So now I know two who betray. And I have the power of life and death in my hands. You should be glad I am nothing." The father kept silent. So the son went on, "You think they will reward you with your olive grove. That they will pay you enough and let you buy it back. And you will have an olive grove among the enemy. And live your old age in peace. You think your own people have lost their sense of smell? The two women were talking about you that night. You could not hear what they decided, but you could hear they were talking about you. And you think children don't have ears? The other woman was the teller's wife. They were going to take you and him away from here, not turn you in. They were going to take you both across the river where you would have to earn your livelihood with some honor. But you thought they might tell on you. So you told the mad mind of this town that the teller's wife had a settler for a lover and he was learning things from her in return for money in the fields. People had just to look at her clothes. Her clothes came from this money, and she found out."

"You are an accomplice," the father said, "you have known a long time, and you have eaten my bread. Your life goes out with mine!" He was smiling bitterly but triumphantly. "Right," the son said, "I go out with you, and you go out with me." The father was livid again because he saw what the son meant. "You never let her give you this choice," the son continued. "I have eaten your bread until I could grow and give you her choice. We either go in the ground together as broken as those two women. Or we go across that river and we live their lives." The father spat his hatred across the wooden table. He reached for a sharp rock to throw but the son reached him first and tore the rock away from him, then gave him a shove down the pathway toward the road into the village. He shoved him again, a few yards at a time. At one spot, the father turned and pointed to the olive grove which he was losing sight of. He shouted to the son, "That is mine!" "You killed it!" the son shouted back. "She was a dog!" the father shouted. "Then you were a dog's lover!" the son shouted back. The father looked for a weapon but the son was on him to bat it out of his hand and give him another shove.

They were now on the road to the village and visible to people. The father knew it so he walked ahead with brief glances back over his shoulder to see how close the son was. "I go out with you," the son kept repeating, "or you go out with me." "You are afraid to die," the father said in a compressed, over the shoulder burst, "I will stop in this village. And you will take your dog's tail across the river. And I will say you had to run." "I will shove you from here to the end of the world and you can tell them what you want," the son answered, "but they will hear me too, and they will not wait to think."

The father made a quick move to his right into the rock and scrub of the roadside, then scrambled down the slope in the direction of the olive grove now well above them. He began to run as best he could towards it but the son caught him and dragged him down. He ripped himself free and ran up the slope with the son behind him. A settler from above fired a warning shot at the two who were acting so strangely, a shot out of the olive grove. But the two men knew only one another in the scramble up the side of that goat pasture. A second shot took the father down, and a third one hit the son as he looked up to make sense of the shooting, hit him in the shoulder and knocked him back. He got up and raised his hand toward the olive grove to stop the shooting, but at the distance of a hundred yards his hand looked like a weapon. So the settler shot him again, this time to death.

The settler radioed for a patrol. The patrol found that the father was still alive. And speaking when they stopped his wound. "It is mine," he said, "the grove is mine. He did not want it. He is a dog. All the dogs are dead." The settler had come down to see. He and the patrol recognised something. So quickly and deftly, they unstopped the father's wound and stood back a bit as if afraid, busy on their walkie-talkies, then they spread out in defensive formation as if there would be others who might attack them. After a few hours, during which they were watched from a distance, they felt safe. They put the two dead men in body bags and delivered them to the village for identification and burial.

2nd Sunday After Christmas

Hunter and Hunted

No one has ever seen God.
—John 1:18

A woman's child was born deformed and not given more than a few years. Her husband simply fled her into a world he could be sure of, good income, golf, and singles bars. She took the baby home and for fourteen months gave the child night and day care until it simply failed in its fragility. A boy she had named Flick. She was part Sioux and that was a name from her past for the quickly disappearing thing, the flick of a wing, of a horse's flanks, of lightning, of a lizard's tongue.

When she had Flick buried she thought it was not enough, a Mass in white, a song of resurrection, a psalm and a sprinkle of holy water at a gravesite. Part of the universe was deformed. And it happened randomly. And the world was like her husband, it just left, and lived as close to beautiful form as it could. She knew as she walked away from that grave of her son that she was facing divinity, not the world that ran. "You will tell me," she said softly within herself, "or you will lose me." So she began to listen, even though she had to lead a noisy life teaching several grades in a multilingual school. She had managed to learn one of the tribal languages of southeast Asia, and there were 24 of that tribe in her school, so she was full time and teaching every subject, bringing them into English from their own tongue. And it looked as though she would have to be again the one room schoolmarm of prairie days. But she was in her soul like a Sioux scout at night and still tracking by sound and smell, and no noise, downwind of the animals, and like a ghost.

The first thing she heard that was not from this world was a gasp. She was up in the hills at a pullout in the road from which she could see sunset and the Pacific Ocean. The sun had just disappeared. It was as if a breath

30

rose, but it was a gasp, like that of soda pop opened. A grief came over the woman. It was more than her own for Flick. And there was the sound of soft hissing that followed the gasp, down to silence, as with soda pop. And her grief left her. The smallest joy in the world replaced it, like the brush of Flick's hand the few times he had seemed to respond. "Do not use me against myself, please," she said.

The second thing she heard that was not from this world was a music. It was a blustery evening outside her home. She was correcting papers of the little ones, their matching up of symbols with things. She had a wind chime on the back porch inside the screens, near her bedroom window. She heard it all night some way, its charming, random patterns, and it added to the depth of her sleep. Right now it sounded tormented, pushed beyond its own gentleness. Then beyond the wind chime she heard the other music, something endless and not dependent on the wind, something so painful it stung her like a hit crazybone, and she almost said no, but gripped herself in time to hear a few more random, infinite beats. Something caused this sound. It was like a voice, the sound came from within the chime. So the woman spoke. "He was not too small." The infinite music ceased instantly. She knew why. She got up from her desk, knelt on the floor and lowered her forehead to her knees, then put her hands out along the floor palms upward. Like the Sioux for rain. Her own wind chimes continued in their tormented sound. But at a moment after a time the other music returned with a few infinite notes, a voice again from within something, but a chime. The woman straightened and put her hands on her thighs. Then she said, "I know this. You have heard me. And him. Who could only scream." She rose and went back to her correcting.

The third thing she heard was in a woman's voice, a woman who waited outside her classroom and asked to see her after dismissal. She sat the woman at a pupil's desk, she sat at another, and heard a story fearfully similar to her own. This athletic, freckled faced, sandy haired woman had a child affected the same way as the teacher's and her husband had left them for similar reasons. The mother could not cope alone. The teacher listening heard an echo voice behind the one speaking to her, a voice asking, "What shall I do?" to no one in particular, just as thunder in a storm is to no one in particular. She was able to help the woman in front of her, able to promise time to her, over the phone, visits, whatever she could.

The child would be gone soon. The teacher then went home to do her homework, but she almost couldn't breathe, the echo voice, she heard it as if she herself had shouted into the canyon. "I do not want my answer," she said in a choked voice as she turned the key to the apartment. "That's *my* answer, 'What shall I do?'"

The fourth thing she heard was her husband's voice. Asking how she was, in a friendly, offhanded way, giving her a chance if she wished to vent her anger for a bit, but she sensed his finger poised over the cutoff buttons. She was very polite, however reserved. She could sense some self-confidence come back into his voice, a certain rightness, the kind he had when he lined up a golf shot or put a check in his pocket without looking at the amount. She sensed someone was watching her from outside this world. Then someone right next to her. Then someone who came inside her and fitted her perfectly. She said goodbye to her husband, "talk to you again, yes, no, don't need anything, bye, bye."

"Oh you!" she said to whomever it was inside her, "what right . . ?" The someone began to leave. She could feel the flush of embarrassment. So she crossed her arms quickly in an embrace and the leaving stopped and reversed and was back fitted to her self and calming. "You do not know either," she said, and she moved toward the kitchen to make some tea. "Why do you not leave all this?" she said. Then after a while, "If you did, I could." She sat to drink. "Nowhere," she said. "That's where he was. Nowhere." Then her cup was empty, a few leaves at the bottom. "You tell me," she said to the leaves at the bottom, then "Ah!" in a gasp, and she leaned back in her chair and spoke to the someone inside her, "We're helpless. The two of us. We know it and he didn't. And we still know it, and he still doesn't. And you will when I'm gone. Nowhere. Then what for you? Someone else you fit in?" She stopped again. And her heart nearly stopped also. "You should not be so foolish," she said, "it's lovely what you offer, but it's foolish." She was standing now. "For you to die is something else." And now she couldn't stand. She could not let someone die for her. And then she could. But said, "Not until I tell you. Please." She rose and rinsed her cup.

Scotching Scorpions

Arise, shine out, Jerusalem, for
your light has come. The glory of
the Lord is rising on you, though
night still covers the earth and
darkness the peoples.
—Isaiah 60:1-2

A woman was watching two scorpions fight. They had hidden in her two shoes while she slept. This was harvest time and she worked as a helper in a kibbutz. Then back to teaching school in town. She had automatically shaken her shoes before she put them on, and out came the scorpions, detected one another, and began this incredible parry and thrust that could be accompanied by mouth harp music. One finally stung the other to death. The woman raised the heel of her shoe and brought it down on the victor with a bang that left it dead too. The other women in the hut were stirring, for breakfast and a day's work, two less scorpions to worry about. "I kill now," the woman thought. "Two years ago I shoveled scorpions out the window into the desert garden. When I had a husband." She took the dead scorpions in her hands, they were like eaten crabs, and dumped them in the trash near the door. She stepped outside in her pajamas still damp from her sleep.

The orange groves seemed to be everywhere in the early light, there was mist rising, the soil still had moisture, but she could see the oranges thick in the trees. She had seen orchards like this suddenly laced with machine gun fire, not for long, three or four terrorists holed up and no chance to survive, only a chance to take someone out with them. Her husband. With his strong curly hair that made his yarmulke look like a baby gorilla riding its mothers shoulders. No baby between them. She heard a

33

honk to her right, the geese, walking their heads on long poles, the perfect watchdogs, they were headed for her for food, soon they'd be stabbing at her thighs. "You're not Zeus, not to me," she said, and she threatened them with a stick near the door. They reversed course and went back towards the kitchen. The door opened behind her and another woman came out, breathed, said, "You'll get cramps undressed," then went off herself towards the kitchen. The light was growing and the tingle of chill on her skin refreshing. "I will leave this," she said to herself, "this is insanity, loveliness held at gunpoint. Let them go crazy and kill one another, then we kill the survivor, but forget he left a nest." She went in and dressed for work. "I want someplace where I can decide what's worth life and death," she thought.

A siren went off. The alarm. "Damn," she shouted and reached under her bed for her weapon. As she brought it out there was another scorpion on the barrel, so she flicked it off onto the floor and gave it a stomp, then she was out the door jamming a clip in her gun, her head swiveling for directions. There was someone pointing to a field they kept free for hay on the other side of the orchard. In a very trained movement about thirty men and women of the kibbutz began a sweep through the orchard toward the field, as if swinging a gate, to be sure no one was behind them. Finally they came to the field and the patrol that had given the alarm. There were two hang gliders out in the field, not quite hidden by the tall grass. "We call in armor," the kibbutz leader said, "run up and down that field a few times. No sense burning good fodder." So he called for armored cars, meantime stretching his group so they surrounded the field. "They're gone somewhere," a voice suggested. "Gone towards town and some school." "School's out, so hospital." Another said, "Did we check the trees enough?" "I need to be sure of that field," the leader said.

Soon the armored cars appeared, crossed into the field and began a run toward the grounded gliders. There was a huge explosion that flipped the first armored car over on its turret. It teetered back on its side then and began to burn as the crew struggled out of the hatch, wounded pulling wounded. The second armored car stopped and turned its turret toward its sister. From behind it, a man rose in the tall grass and ran to fling himself against it. There was another explosion as the human bomb dove against the side of the vehicle, another flipped vehicle, and this time the kibbutzim ran into the field to pull the personnel out of the ruined car. There couldn't be a third bomber? The woman found herself stamping through the grass, her weapon on automatic, until they had the grass flattened and were sure there was no one else. But there were bits and pieces of human flesh hanging from nearly all the stalks. It took a long time to clear the field. It was afternoon before they could get back in the trees and resume harvesting the oranges. The oranges. Bits of flesh hanging in the trees. The woman leaned her kerchiefed head against the branch she was picking. "I am right, we are right, they are right. The only one who is wrong is the one who loses."

She descended the ladder and went to the barn where she got a tank of kerosene and a backpack sprayer, for use in burning away thistles along the roads. She went to the head of the kibbutz and said, "I am going to burn that field. There is flesh in there. We feed it to no one." He shrugged his assent. She knew he was not a believer, that his assent was practical. So she went upwind and began to burn the field, keeping the fire moving in a line. Luckily the smoke drifted away from the orchard. But people noticed and some came to tend it with her. The army had taken the hang gliders away, and had hauled off the wrecked armored cars. So she burned the whole field until it was a blackened rectangle. Then she went out and sat in the middle of it, the ashes still hot through her Levis. "Whoever you are," she said in a prayer to God, "this is what we are. You should not tell us things. We know enough on our own."

She saw in the ashes near her a burned scorpion half in, half out of its hole in the ground. She flicked some ashes and dirt away with her smudged fingers, then pulled the shell out. There were small live ones in the hole who had been saved by the dead one blocking the entrance. "I can do my part again," she said aloud, "I can kill the killers." "Leave them," the kibbutz leader said behind her, "or we'll have too many beetles. And less oranges. So less money. And less security. You understand? Now come." "Why did you let me burn the field?" she asked. "There's less fodder." "I don't know," he said, "gets rid of the funny smell maybe."

The Baptism of the Lord

Savage Grace

See, I have made you a witness to
the peoples, a leader and a master
of the nations.
——Isaiah 55:4

A bear had mauled some campers. The ranger knew which one. Last few times the animal had only frightened people. They had air-lifted it out nice and drugged and set it loose far from camp areas, but it had drifted back late in the season, hundreds of miles, a rare thing. Lucky for the people mauled that there was food left carelessly near the tent. That had brought the bear in the first place. And their panic and pot and pan rattling had set the animal swinging some lethal claws which had left people scarred and running through underbrush while the bear went back to eating. The ranger had to kill it, it had learned what could not be unlearned. But he couldn't risk not killing it, having it wounded and on the loose. So he would have to herd it out of the valley and up towards the hills. In a few days, camping season would be over. And shortly thereafter the first snows and the signal to the bear's system to find its hibernation cave. So he would have to move quickly.

He packed well, light tent, down roll, cold food only, no stove, transmitter/receiver. It was really a one man job. He started from the scene of the last reported attack, the day before yesterday, found paw prints, they were heading west, toward several campsites up the face of the valley slope. He covered the ground fairly quickly, reporting in over radio his position and destination. The first campsite was a wreck, but the campers had been experienced and knew how to leave a bear be. Three men, but they said this was a mean bear and it had acted out of a rage more than a hunger. The men were saving what they could and heading in. The next campsite was

36

just hours after being wrecked. Two men this time, at their breakfast, they simply retreated, doing the smart thing, dropping bits of food then clothing to distract the animal, then running across the stream and downslope alongside it until they were sure of no pursuit. They only returned when they saw the bear actually break cover far above them on its way to the spine of the ridge. The ranger phoned in the incident, left the men to return to the lodge, then began upstream in pursuit of the animal. His rifle was high powered, with telescope, but off came the telescope, he had to go close in and use visual sighting. The bear must not leave. There was one more campsite in the uphill direction, then two below on some lookout promontories, no water there obviously, but not far down to it.

"I'll have to get him coming down," the ranger thought. "The wind is his way. I'll bring him down on myself." So the ranger went cross slope, checked the two promontory campsites, they were empty, and clean, so no attraction. But the bear would soon get wind of him. The ranger went to the furthest out of the sites, opened some cans of food and dumped their contents on the ground yards out leading in the direction of the camp. He took a nylon rope and tied it around the base of a pine tree near the lip of the drop. It was forty feet down, he could go most of it on the rope if his bullets failed. No bear would jump. His gun was loaded. Power enough to kill any animal.

The bear showed. About forty yards away upslope in the trees. The ranger squatted and waited. He was actually sad. It was a great animal out there, this was its territory, but you could not explain it. It was moving for the man, slowly, around the trees, face on mostly. When cover gave out it would charge. Exactly what it did. The ranger's first shot almost halted it, the bullet was so powerful, but the bear began again. The second shot did halt it, its breath gone, its throat pouring blood into its lungs. It reared, not fifteen yards away, so the third shot took its heart out and it fell. There was never any doubt, the ranger knew, what with this gun. Tying the escape rope had been a bit of superstition.

The ranger waited crouched, gun still ready, the involuntary jerking of the carcase stopped. He lowered his rifle, reached for his radio, and called in where he was and with whom. Control said a helicopter and sling would come in and bring them out. "Be sure it's dead," Control ordered as it signed off. "All right, one more shot," the ranger said. He aimed between the eyes and squeezed the trigger and took much of the head away with the bullet. Then he lowered the gun. "Forgive me," he said to the bear. He stood up and looked for the shells, found them, they had not gone over the cliff, put them in his pocket, then walked past the bear and cleaned the trail of food, threw that over the precipice for smaller animals to eat. Then stood looking for the helicopter to come.

"I have to keep this place savage," he thought, "so people can taste the raw life." Then, "I should not have fired that last bullet. I broke something. I am alone here." It was as if he could no longer read; trees, wind, light, sounds, had turned into a strange alphabet. "I can force them," he thought, "that is what I'll have to do. I am now a master." The shots had stilled all life in the woods.

So he heard the growl and whipped around into a crouch, rifle to his shoulder, the shock of surprise clearing his senses like ammonia. Beyond the dead bear was another. The ranger had seen only one set of tracks, had only one set of reports. The live bear was at the carcass of the other, swaying back and forth and growling, at the ranger. "Shoot now," the ranger thought. But he didn't. He let the bear move first if it moved. And it did move, not in a charge, but almost in a cat stalk toward him. He still did not shoot. The bear stopped ten yards away. Out of the corner of his eye the ranger saw the cubs move back up in the trees. "I can take the rope," he thought. He was eye to eye with that animal. One shot and he was safe. One foot closer and there'd be no shot. But he needed something back that would be lost forever if he fired. The bear looked to either side, the first break in the confrontation, then it wheeled around itself and looked back. The ranger lowered his rifle slowly, scarcely moving. The bear wheeled around itself again, looked again, then turned and went back, nosing the dead carcass briefly, up into the trees and its cubs.

The ranger rose from his crouched position and stayed facing the woods, not the vista, and the elements began to speak again, but with caution, as if he were still on trial. "It is better this way," he said. "Better you tell me. Or I have only this." He put his gun on the ground and hunkered down to wait for the chopper.

One Stupid Grape

Spare your people, Lord! Do not make
your heritage a thing of shame!
—Joel 2:17

"There are little sins and big sins," a woman thought as she took a grape from a bunch on the stand in a supermarket and tasted it. "Mmm, not quite ripe." They were green grapes and she shouldn't touch them at all, the boycott was still on. "What for this time?" she asked herself. "O, working conditions," she answered. There had been a chemical taste. "They're worried about birth defects." "What a weight!" she thought then. "I just swallowed a crime, I think." "Potatoes are okay. All done by machine. The nice long rows in Maine and Idaho dug up and spewed out then scooped into bags that smell fresh dirt all the way to the supermarket. Eat a peck of dirt and it makes no monster in the belly." "Ah," she thought, "the babies that come out addicts! Eat a peck of crack!" She looked up to the heavens and said, "What's all this? I just took a grape and you're dumping the cosmos on me!"

She moved toward the lettuce. "Which kind is forbidden? Iceberg. Okay, why? I don't know. Maybe some rights violations. Look at it, it's really crisp and fresh as spring water. Sorry, iceberg. You go the way of all flesh!" She took some romaine. Then she squeezed a few peaches. Not ready yet. She found a thumb hole in one of them. Somebody wanted to be absolutely sure. Somebody with AIDS, and a cut thumb, and here was a time bomb waiting to happen in someone's mouth. "O cripes!" she thought, "do I know anything?" Strawberries then. From Mexican fields. Fields that should be growing wheat. Not serving foreign palates. "Okay, but people get paid. My mind's gone nuts!" She let out a snort of exasperation. "One grape, one stupid damn grape and I'm wired into every-thing that's wrong." She looked back along the fruit and produce section. She saw another woman test the grapes as she looked over the whole section. She took one. Then she took another while swiveling her head from one side to the other. She took a third, then pushed her cart a few feet, took some potatoes, tossed them in the basket, went back and took a few more grapes, then pulled some plastic sacks off the roll and started to feel through the peaches. The woman watching could sense the squeezes, they were that hard. "She's free," the woman watching thought, "that hurts too. I better leave the planet."

She turned her own cart down the coffee aisle. Her husband loved Nescafé, heavy cream, sugar, stirred together before the hot milk. "Nice Nestlés," she thought, "you and the babies you killed with your powdered milk. Really, the dirty water those women were too dumb to understand. Ah!" she said as she stamped her foot to get rid of a thought. "If I didn't know! If I just grew out of a belly and off some tits into a naked land and flies in my eyes, I wouldn't suspect either. This place is a bible." She rounded the corner into pharmaceuticals. Two racks of condoms. Romantic colors, romantic names, heros and heroines. Two racks of aspirin. One a day keeps cardiacs away. "O, just bread now. And some milk. And some cheese." She came to the checkout counter. She had eight items, right for the first lane. As the cashier rang up her things, she said to her, "Take out an extra nickel." The cashier laughed, "You eat a grape?" "Yes," the woman answered. "I will if it was ripe," said the cashier. "It wasn't," said the woman. "So no nickel," said the cashier, "we will sell no grape before its time." "You shouldn't be selling those grapes at all," said the woman, "so take out a nickel and drop it in the heart box." "Okay, two nickels," the cashier said. "Now the world's right," the woman said, "and we did it." "You're a breath," said the cashier. "Some people want to lynch me. And some people right behind them want to cut me down and string the others up. Here, I'll bag these for you. The old guy is out for a smoke. They're good, the old guys, they learned how to work. There's some pride." "They never asked questions," the woman said. She and the cashier had their hands on the bag. "They couldn't live if they did," the cashier said as she let go of it. "I do, and I walk out with the same bag of groceries," the woman said. The cashier turned to the next customer. Like someone who had come to the bottom of a dead end street.

The woman lifted her purchases and headed outside. There was a point where the automatic door was triggered. She stopped just short of it. Someone passed and triggered it open. She stayed where she was. Someone else passed. "We're on automatic," she thought. "I am. When I go off automatic, I can't move." She recognised a woman go by her, the grape eater. This time she was breaking the end off a loaf of french bread stuck in the top of her full cart. She was a thin woman and the kind that would stay thin if her mouth were never empty. "I'll walk you to your car, have a smoke myself," the cashier said as she came up behind her. "Isn't there some non-automatic door we can go through?" the woman asked. "Fire door," said the cashier, "but it brings the world howling down on you. Come on!"

The two passed the critical point and the door jerked open. Out they went into the lot. A truck was just pulling past leaving a cloud of diesel exhaust for them to breathe. They both held their breaths until the black cloud lifted. Then the cashier laughed. "I smoke too. Don't stand too close." They crossed to the parking slots. Then stopped in the sunlight. "Cancer," the cashier said as she looked up at the sun. Then they both just roared. "We're in it aren't we?" said the woman. "Up to our necks. A sin if we do. A sin if we don't." "Okay, no more cigarettes," said the cashier as she dropped the one she was smoking and stepped on it. "No more grapes," said the woman. "No more sex," said the cashier. "Wait," said the woman, "no need to be fanatic." "Okay, never with strangers," the cashier said. "Yes," said the woman, "make friends first." And they both were actually crying and very serious. "Nobody lets you love," the cashier said and she was looking back up towards the sun, "somebody ruins the grapes." "I ruin your day," the woman said. "It should happen all the time. Like this. Not like those doors," the cashier said. "I gotta go. The old guy can't see the numbers on the register. Fast line becomes slow line. See you." "Hope to," said the woman as she put her groceries on the hood and unlocked her car.

There was a flyer stuck under the windshield wiper blocking her view. She freed it. It said "JESUS SAVES," and gave a number to phone. She tore it into small pieces, confetti like, held it in the palm of her hand and let the light breeze blow it all away. Then she noticed the sign on one of the abandoned carts. "DO NOT LITTER." "Say please," she said, and got into her car.

Hot Pursuit

Now it was long ago, when Noah was
building that ark which saved only
a small group of eight people by
water, and when God was still
waiting patiently, that these
spirits refused to believe.
—1 Peter 3:20

A man had his pocket picked. Cute the way it was done. A flower girl
with a tray of carnations, large tray with a strap to go around her neck and
hold the edge under her bosom. Her blouse was open and her new breasts
showed. Her sister, half her size and age, walked beside her holding on to
her long skirt. The older one walked right up to the man and put the tray
gently against him and asked him to buy a flower. He said no, with a
smile, and moved around her, the opposite side to the small girl whom he
had lost sight of due to the tray.

A few minutes later he sensed his pocket was light. A hot fury set in,
he ran back along the streets he had walked, then did a search through
neighboring streets and alleys until he saw the two from behind, saw them
work another man, the little girl quick as a snake's tongue had the wallet
out of the man's back pocket and inside the bosom of her blouse, the older
girl kept the man engaged even as he said no, holding the tray against him
as he walked around the two exactly as the one who was watching did.
Then he saw the next step, the little girl had the wallet back out, the paper
money removed, and the wallet scaled under a nearby parked car with a
quick flip of the wrist. "So my wallet's under a car," the man thought. The
paper money went into the older girl's skirt pocket. "There's probably a
man around," the victim thought. "Someone who can hit hard and run if

43

anybody catches the two." He looked. Yes, a bum-like figure with a plastic sack over his shoulder, small sack with a couple of telltale bulges, cans of food maybe, enough to ring someone's skull and look innocent afterwards. Everybody could escape in the confusion.

"The little girl is the key," he thought, "if I can just break her wrist." So he rumpled his clothes a bit, rearranged his tie, took his appointment book from his suitcoat and put it in his rear pocket, got out ahead of the flower girl and her kid sister, turned and walked back toward them, but in a preoccupied way, maybe they wouldn't recognize him and would try for another hit. They did, he felt the tray come softly up against him, the little girl disappeared from view. He said no, and as he did he grabbed for his own back pocket and closed on the soft wrist of the flicking hand of the little girl and held it. He knew where the man was. The little girl gave him a fierce kick in the shins but he snapped her around with a twist of her arm and he put his other hand right in her hair and knotted the two together. The sack man started to move, then stopped when he saw he was spotted. The scene might look affectionate, a man holding a little girl by the head and by the hand talking to a young woman with a tray of flowers. "I just break this arm," the man said. "So take out my forty dollars and lay them on the tray." The little girl squirmed. The older girl took out the forty dollars. The man's eyes were fixed on the sack man and they were fierce with anger. But the hot flesh feel of the little girl hit him harder than her kick. Whatever she was, she was flesh and blood. And the money on the tray of flowers in front of him was not. He loosed his grip and stepped quickly back. A terrible coldness had come over him. And a sense of foolishness. Then a sense of humiliation. The woman dropped the money on the street and moved sideways away from him. The man saw this but also saw the other man move quickly with his sack ready for a hit. They had everything calculated, even revenge. He let the money lie on the ground as he stared at the other man. The money began to move down the street in little tumbles. The man with the sack wavered just a bit, his eyes flicked aside. The game was over. The man with the sack quickly picked up the sliding bills, stuffed them in a pocket and moved across the street with absolute scorn written across his face.

"Forty stinking bucks!" the man who had been robbed thought, "you can buy the use of a kid for that!" Then, "I can't buy anything, I'm stripped!" He started to walk back toward the albergo where he was staying. And his humiliation increased. He passed what he could not buy, coffee, books, postcards, shirts, shoes. "I'd have to ask," he thought, as he passed people you could not ask. "Or I'd have to steal. If you give up power you are helpless." He felt himself beginning to collapse inside. A woman's voice broke through and asked him, "Do you know where Canal Street is?" "No," he said, "sorry." And she said, "Could you help me find it?" He put both hands in his pockets and pulled them out so they were like the ears of a dog. "Oh," she said, "you're impotent." And she moved away from him to look for more Canal Streets." "If I go back and bash that kid I'm not," he thought. But he felt that warm wrist in his hand, and the warm skull through the hair he held in his grip, and he saw the young woman peeking through her own blouse, the tray of flowers that hid the theft, the money doing back flips down the street in the light wind. "That's impotence," he thought, "it burns."

"You in trouble, buddy?" a voice said at his shoulder. He was waiting for a light to change. "Run something for me and I'll put your pockets back in." The man realized his pockets were still out, like a beggar, not a dog. "Just ran," he answered the voice. "Cops caught me. They're using me as bait. Photograph anyone who talks to me." The voice at his shoulder simply muttered, "Then you're dead," and left.

Hot fury gripped the man again. He held for a minute against it, then turned and started through the crowd after the voice. Then stopped. There was the voice with a tray of flowers being pushed gently against his chest and a small hand flicking a wallet out of his back pocket while the voice with both hands was shoving the tray and the older girl aside. The wallet was stripped and flung under a car and the money popped down the pocket of the older girl's skirt. But the voice sensed the lifted wallet, turned and made a grab for the older girl shouting curses at her. The man with the sack of cans stepped out of a doorway and hit the voice over the head and ran. The girls got free, the voice howled from his knees, and the man watching all this grinned, then hit his own face with hand, but couldn't hold back. He went up to the kneeling voice and said, "You in trouble, buddy?"

2nd Sunday, Lent

'Nam Chaplain

*Could anyone accuse those that God
has chosen? When God acquits, could
anyone condemn?*
—Romans 8:33-4

"I have to tell you I hate the story of Abraham and Isaac," a priest said to a congregation the Sunday the passage from *Genesis* had to be read. "I know that God had no intention of going through with the demand that Abraham sacrifice Isaac. But Abraham had every intention of obeying. So we are descendants of someone who would do anything God asked. 'O, God will ask only good things from then on,' you say. 'And God only wanted to show Abraham that God was not a tyrant like earthly kings.'" The priest waited a minute, moving the book a bit on its stand in the pulpit. "Maybe its really a case of people putting demands in God's mouth. Maybe what the writer of *Genesis* was doing was frightening people first, that God could ask such a thing, then assuring them that God really could not. But look at that pitiful creature Abraham who had a miracle of a son born to the old age of himself and his wife, and now he had to kill the miracle so far as he knew. He should have said, 'No, God, it is not like you, something has happened to you.'"

There was uneasiness in the congregation. "Maybe I'm ruined as a preacher," the priest went on, "maybe I can now only see things through my experience of Vietnam. I should never have agreed to be a chaplain for that war." There was a groan in the congregation, one that seemed both against and for what the priest had said. "One time when I was back on leave, I was asked to go to a high school run by religious and to represent the pro-war viewpoint on a discussion day held by the senior class. I wore my paratrooper boots and my insignia and my bronze star and purple heart.

My hair was cut combat style. And I explained patriotic conscience to those seniors and told them to serve when called, that duty would not betray them and that God would honor what they did. When I went back to the war, I used to do the same thing, tell troubled marines that God would honor what they did, tell them to go back into combat, and that the death they caused unintentionally was not to be blamed on them. They hated me afterwards, though I never knew this directly, most avoided me. I was a 'Nam' chaplain. I tried to stay in but that was an illusion. God did not honor what we did."

There were more groan-like sounds from the congregation, for him, against him. "All right, I shouldn't say that either," the priest continued. "I was wrong about God in war, I could be wrong about God in peace. I remember one man coming in to see me, he was on river patrol, he was the gattling gunner, you know, those guns with many barrels tied together in a bundle and the bundle spins so huge bullets get spewed out in a stream but no one barrel overheats. A man could cut a hole in a wall of trees with that gun. And he said to me, 'I love it, it's like a climax in love-making. I love this whole war, and that can't be right. Do it but don't love it, isn't that right, Padre?' And I said yes, do it, but don't love it, and if you do love it, be sorry that you do."

"Now look at me," the priest said to the congregation. "I'm Abraham. But Abraham without God stopping me! God killed Abraham that day. Really. Abraham was just a stud. I look at my offspring—yes, those soldiers are my offspring—and I realize that they had to come to a different faith than mine or they were lost. And you know many of them were. You see them hugging one another at the Vietnam wall in Washington as though they were survivors of a shipwreck in which all their goods and family went down. I went there last week. I wore my combat jacket with the chaplain's insignia. I know there are names on that wall of people I met, but I couldn't connect with any one specific name. And no one came near me. No one came near the chaplain. No man, that is.

A nurse did. Psychiatric nurse. She said, 'Padre, you're in the wrong place.' She said it sympathetically. She put her arm through mine and she began to walk me up the incline. 'You're judging me,' I said. 'No,' she said, 'no, I mean there's no cure for you here. What you told them is carved in stone also. The whole happening is frozen here in stone.'

'Where is there a cure for me?' I asked her. 'In that which is not stone,' she said, 'in what you say from now on.' Well, I was speechless and we were at the top of the path, out on the Mall. Then she said, 'I helped send them back into combat also. I helped spot the fakers.' I never held a woman in my life the way I held her, I thought she was going to disintegrate right there and disintegrate me with her. But time helps, even a few minutes time. It's been a week since she left me standing, a week since I've come home, a week since I've done all the parish things you see me do, a week since I've had to face the Scriptures for this Sunday, and then face you with something to say. I sacrificed my son on that mountain. The angel of mercy did not reach me in time. Do you see that I played both God and Abraham? And that I hate this Scripture because it reminds me now? But I am not the angel of mercy. Not to myself. It is always someone else. Like the woman who came up to me. She didn't have to. And I didn't have to listen.

"*We* speak the voices, my dear people. If we pretend there is any other voice to God but mercy . . ." the priest paused, then went on ". . . I don't know what to say to finish that sentence . . . we will have no sons? no daughters? no destiny but to be like sand on the seashore, not countless, but lifeless and caught between wind and wave? I am sorry for imposing this sermon on you. But she said words are not stone. I can be reached with words, you can reach me if I am wrong. I just ask you to remember that though you call me father, I am also your son, and you speak to me from God."

Woman Under the Influence

You shall have no gods except me.
You shall not make yourself a
carved image or any likeness of
anything in heaven or on earth
beneath or in the waters under the
earth; you shall not bow down to
them or serve them.
                    —Exodus 20:3-4

A woman loved gold. Not the gold itself so much. If you gave her an ingot she would drop it on your toes and say "Ugh!" It was the art of gold, what it drew artisans to do. The halos and angel hair done by Beato Angelico were exquisite. And the religious masks done by the Incas also. Some few survived the smelting. So she became an expert on the art of gold. But that was not enough. She became an artisan, learning how to do her own smelting, make her own molds, and eventually her own designs, though she fell far short of some of the classic work. She supported herself mainly by doing jewelry repair. She repaired some pretty ghastly stuff. Though some things were almost too elegant for her touch.

One was an all gold chalice stenciled with vine and grapes all around the cup. The stem was moulded to seem like the trunk of a vine. And the base shaped like clods of earth to support the vine. The chalice had been crushed by something, bent badly out of shape. It would almost have to be melted then redone. But the owner didn't want that. He was a retired priest who had spent years working in an old Spanish mission station and among Indians converted by force or fraud to Christianity. The chalice must have been in a trunk at the mission. She had her doubts about the rightful ownership. Well, the Church anyway, and the priest was part of it.

49

So she cleaned the gold first, using dentist's equipment. She saw how lovely it was, yet it looked like native work, a native artisan perhaps, copying some European model printed in a book. The vine looked more like nettles and the grapes more like thistle blossoms. In fact, that is what they were! Nettles and thistle blossoms! So what was the stem? The more she looked at the stem—and it was thick and had a knob she had thought was a knot, to make handling the chalice easier—the more she sensed it was the navel of a twisted torso. It was a female twisted torso and in some degree pregnant. So what was the ground below the torso? Not clods. As she cleaned, she saw they were infant heads. The backs. As if they were dead. Yet it took close inspection to see what she saw. An ordinary glance would see vine, grapes, trunk, and ground. She was looking at a subtle optical illusion, all bent out of shape, but glowing with the beauty of gold.

The woman knew she was in love with this object. She began to spend every waking minute working on it, reporting to the priest that she would try to restore it to as near perfection as she could, that it was pure gold, and it would take time. He was hesitant and asked would the restoration cost more than the chalice was worth. It was just a souvenir of his days at the mission. "I will do it without cost," she said, "I find it lovely, and I will tell you it will be very precious when I get through." "What do you mean?" he asked. "I mean it's pure gold," she said, "solid gold all the way through. There is no other metal reinforcing it. And it has a design on it that is the most original I have ever seen, and it tells an extraordinary story, I think, about the one who made it, and about the ones who used it." The priest did not respond. She knew what he was thinking. "Padre," she said, "I will weigh this, and I will give you $500 an ounce if you wish, some $30,000. I will give it to you in cash. When I restore the chalice, it will be an artwork you will have to explain. If I give you the money and restore the chalice, you can return it to the mission where it can be put on display. I will write up its meaning. But please do not melt it down." The woman knew she was ready to do something else that would take the chalice out of both their hands. But she loved it and would only report it out of desperation. "Send the money," the Padre said quietly. "Agreed," the woman said.

So she continued the perilous work of restoring the crumpled chalice. She used varying kinds of pressure tools, all of them padded. She used a computer drawing to keep what the original was like before her eyes. She used laser beams to calculate correct angles. Her studio looked like a primitive atom smasher with all the equipment she had. Over a year's time she had the chalice back to its original self, the cup beautifully rounded, the vine/thistle design showing in powerful but subtle line, the twisting torso of the woman. It was with the base that she had had the most trouble. It was difficult to reshape such a large amount of bent solid gold. But it had to be done. The chalice was a glorious thing. She heated it as much as she could and applied soft pressure over a period of a month, watching it practically every minute until she was bleary eyed and until the base was perfectly horizontal, aligned with the lip of the cup, and the chalice stood there in its original shape.

It was then she noticed it was dated. With a dating she did not understand. Pictorial. Designs from the Aztec Calendar. She consulted and found the designs to say 1572. So it was a christian Aztec who did this. And it traveled a long way to that trunk in a mission station in the southwest. "I don't want to give this up," she thought. "This is gold speaking someone's soul." The Padre could never really claim it. He took it without someone's permission, and no explanation would really cover him. He was old, and he wanted peace his last years. And Indians had no use for gold. Someone would steal and sell this and it would go into a crucible and come out flat and vicious. And she had paid for it. "But I'll have to keep it to myself," she thought. "I can't give it back to him. When he knows what this chalice really says he may melt it himself. To think that the wine of God was blessed in this for three centuries and this was screaming no! no! you are killing *me*, not Jesus, for your soul's salvation! Your god is gold!" She thought more, "I don't have to tell him. I can say it's awkward work by a native artist a long time ago. I can photograph this every way possible. Art shots. I can show him the photos. That will keep the chalice in existence." She was looking at it with passion that heated her cheeks, her mind fashioning ways to be sure this object of art stayed in the world in its beautiful form. "If I let this go, I let myself go," she concluded. Then, "I have to let it go. The Aztec did. He had one bloodthirsty god after another."

It was then she saw there was another level of meaning to the chalice. The heads of the dead children seemed to be *rising*. And the body of the woman seemed to be *untwisting*. And the mouth of the chalice seemed to be thirsting for wine, not blood. Wine from thistles and thorns. She had almost failed to see. Gold fever could blind you. Art fever could blind you. To what someone was revealing. "Oh, how beautiful!" she said aloud. She was not talking to the chalice. She was talking to someone who made it. Someone long gone. She photographed the chalice. She phoned the Padre and told him it was ready, he could return it to the mission for display. Something restored at his expense. She would do the writeup and publish it. He hesitated. Then said, almost so she couldn't hear it, "I will publish the writeup." She knew what he was saying, it was his best cover for taking the chalice. "All right," she said, "you publish. But I deliver." She waited for him to think this through. "Yes," he said, "because you did what I wanted done." "I did," she said. "And you are younger and can travel," he said. "I am," she said. "And you can explain what I found." "I can," she said. "I will call chancery," he said. "Do," she said, and hung up the phone.

Maniacal Fury

*We are God's work of art, created
in Christ Jesus to live the good
life as from the beginning he had
meant us to live it.*
　　—Ephesians 2:10

A man decided on revenge. For small things, small revenges. For big things, big revenges. Only small things happened to him. Mainly from automobiles. He worked in a downtown area where streets were narrow and drivers savage, either to find parking places, or to make time. His toes were cringing constantly from near misses, cabs especially cut close. And his kneecaps had St. Vitus Dance. His groin shrank for safety's sake everytime he stepped off a curb. So he took to carrying a small can of spray paint in one hand, his brief case in the other with his samples of office supplies. Everytime someone cut too close he would spray their car with a swatch of purple, or pink, or beet red, a quick flip of the hand, finger on nozzle. The driver would notice later and feel as helpless as he felt when they used their car on him as a weapon.

One van truck nearly killed him with its side view mirror, then had to brake for a car pulling out suddenly from the curb. So it sat for a second fat and vulnerable. He made two purple clouds on its rear door, two sweeps of the spray can. If he ever saw a culprit who went by him too closely park down the street a ways, he would wait for the driver to lock and go. Then he would sidle up to the car, take a wooden match, break it in half, and stick the safe half in the air nozzle of the tire so it would go flat slowly and surely over the next twenty minutes. That was a riskier operation. The culprits usually called Triple A, though he at least cost them time.

53

But one day he got sick of himself. Revenge wasn't balancing things out. Traffic wasn't improving. His whole body still trembled when he crossed streets. And the big things, genocides and starvations and air pollution, these were untouchable by any revenge whatsoever. He passed many news stands in a day, so headlines were burned into his eyeballs, as were the breasts and thighs and buttocks of actresses and athletes and body builders. Revenge is suicide he concluded one day. It's like sucking the egg out of its shell and leaving the nice shell. But this was before he actually got hit by a truck, a glancing blow that sent him spinning into the fender of a parked car and sent his briefcase up over the hood and onto the sidewalk where his samples scattered every which way. The truck kept going. And he chased it with maniacal fury.

But some cold reason got into the fury, his bare hands were not enough, a spray can, a broken matchstick were not enough, he needed a fearful weapon to teach that driver what it was nearly to get killed. He had the number of the truck. He needed the face of the driver. So at a cross street, where the truck paused, he simply ran out ahead of it, stopped, and fixed the face of the driver in his memory, not too obviously so the driver would recall when questioned by the police. "I'm going to find out who this guy is," the man thought, "and I'm going to get a car, and I'm going to scare him to the point of death with it." He checked with the company, got the name of the driver through a simple-minded ruse, found out where he lived, then began to track him on days he was off.

He saw his chance one Saturday. The man with a grown son had come out of the house and gone down the street toward a tavern. They had to cross to get to it. "I'd better miss, but miss close," the man thought as he sped up from his cruising speed. Miss he just did, the two of them, who leaped back, then filled the air with cursing. The driver ran a red light and got away. He had muddied his license plate in back, and the car was rented. "I don't think it's enough," he thought, "one scare won't get through." So he hired a van this time. And nearly nailed his victim when the latter was reaching for the door of his truck on a street downtown. The victim tried to give chase in the truck but it was too unwieldy.

The third time a new factor entered. The victim had become suspicious. The man who was laying back in a hired jeep noticed he had a gun in his belt as he got out of his truck warily to go in and get coffee. Same thing when he came out, a careful eye up the street in the direction of traffic and a hand poised near the opening of his coat. "A sucker for someone backing up," the man thought, "but a wild bullet and somebody else gets it." So he eased his jeep forward with the blinker on right as if he was going to fill the parking place the truck would leave. Nonetheless the victim almost pulled the gun. There was rage and hatred written all over his face and absolute intention to kill. He got in the truck and pulled out savagely. Too bad for anyone who got in the way.

The man moved his jeep into the emptied space. "He knows more than I do," he thought. "You don't teach, you don't learn, you kill if you have to, it's accident or self defense. I'm as sick as he is." He sat there for a while, then he noticed in his door mirror that the truck was down behind him several cars away and waiting. If he opened the door to get out, it would be an accident. If he got out on the sidewalk side, it would be an admission and there'd be a shot. If he pulled out, that'd be an admission too, and there'd be an accident he might escape from but with some broken bones. So he started his jeep, put it in reverse so the lights showed in the back, saw the struck start forward. He then shifted into four wheel drive, made a feint left toward the street, then a hard right up on the sidewalk as the truck roared past where he should have been. He reversed the jeep and was back out on the street.

"Can't let him shoot," he thought. "But we know each other now." He rode the jeep forward and out enough so the trucky could see him in his mirror. "He'll have to get out of that cab to shoot. He knows it. Can he do it fast enough?" The man kept sliding his gear shift into neutral, gunning the motor, then putting the shift back into third with a grind of metal. Which told the trucky the jeep was ready. And obsessed. So the trucky didn't see the STOP sign nor the tanker coming into the intersection. The tanker got hit behind the cab and before the tank. And the tank overturned and caught the jeep in the sweep of an arm, and all three, jeep, truck, tanker screeched across the asphalt locked together. And the gasoline in the tanker began to leak out on the ground.

The man caught in the jeep saw the man caught in the truck. One spark and they would both be cremated in a horrible death. And everything within reach of the blast. Eye to eye they saw the same horrible truth. But the man in the jeep could get out. His roof had been sprung. The man in the truck knew it. He had his gun in his hand. As if to say "You move and I spark this thing." So the man in the jeep began to move, to push the cloth roof up more, deliberately, his eyes on the trucky, daring him, as the gasoline leaked more and more onto the street around them. The jeep man leaned across the top of his windshield and slid out onto the crumpled hood that was gripped between the overturned tank and the body of the truck. He climbed slowly onto the tank and worked his way forward to the trucky's crushed cab. Then sat on top of the tank a few feet away and just stared at the man pinned inside.

There were shouts from several directions to run for it, including from the driver of the tanker who had climbed through his own door window and was frantically chasing people away. The siren sounds were rising and the hoots of fire equipment, and people in buildings were being shoved away from windows. But the man from the jeep sat on top of the tank looking at the man trapped in the cab of the truck. And the madness snapped. The trapped man motioned to break the windshield. The jeep man got on the hood of the truck and started to bash in the glass with kicks, it had already been sprung. Then he reached in and began to yank the steering wheel out of the man's chest so he could work free. Water began to descend on the two of them, spouts from several directions. Then foam, then foam-covered men reached them and began to drag them both across horizontal ladders towards safety.

The jeep man saw the trucky drop the gun between the crushed vehicles into the bed of foam. The firemen saw nothing but the rescue. When the two were in the ambulance, the trucky said to the jeep man, "We're even." Just that, flat and empty voice. "We are," the jeep man said, same voice. "Nothing to nothing."

Ugly Eats Beautiful

Now sentence is being passed on
this world; now the prince of this
world is to be overthrown.
—John 12:31

A girl was watching her favorite Saturday cartoon on TV. But things weren't going right. Ugly was catching Beautiful and would soon swallow her alive with his dragon mouth. "Mama!" the girl shouted, in real fear. The Mother came out of the kitchen just in time to see Ugly catch Beautiful and begin to crunch her like a candy bar. The girl started to scream, "No! No!" and so did the mother, and neither thought to hit the off button. They watched Ugly eat Beautiful to death. Then stand there licking his dragon chops in total satisfaction. But then Ugly got a strange look on his face, as if he were being twisted from inside, agony shot through his whole frame and pieces began to fall off him as pieces do off bombed buildings. Then he began to split the way sidewalks do. Finally, in a great roar of grief, he simply disintegrated. And the screen went empty.

The girl and her mother expected to see Beautiful rise as if from sleep, but nothing. Then an ad came on, for a chocolate covered ice cream bar, then an ad for special toothpaste, then an ad for flesh toned bandaids, then an ad for milk. The little girl was whimpering. The mother was furious. She got on the phone to the station, asked for the program manager, heard that the line was busy, could she leave a number. No, she'd call back. Which she did every five minutes, but now could not get through because of a constant busy signal. She had her little girl with her right by the phone and would lift it from her ear so they both could hear the beep-beep. "Everybody's calling. I'll go higher," she said. She looked up the Network number in New York and put a call through. It was Saturday. Leave a message on a machine. "Come on," she said to her little girl, "we'll go down to the station."

There was a crowd at the door when they arrived, angry parents, red-eyed children. And only technicians working the place. So an engineer was out on the front steps trying to explain he had not seen the cartoon first, he just ran it, it came in a cassette from the parent company all ready to go, he just pushed the buttons. "You killed off Beautiful!" one parent shouted. "You ruined these kids." "Didn't do a thing," the technician shouted back, "it's only a dumb cartoon. Beautiful will be back in a week, wherever she's gone. Cartoons are to make money. Just go home, will you! Give your kid a hug. Tell 'em *they're* beautiful!" A howl of protests went up from the listening crowd. And more people were arriving. "And you're Ugly!" someone shouted. "Okay, I'm Ugly," the technician shouted back, "you're Beautiful! So go home!" "Bring back Beautiful, bring back Beautiful," the crowd began to chant, thick voices of parents, thin voices of children.

Suddenly the technician seemed to have an attack of some kind, he put his hands up around his throat as if he couldn't breathe. Then in gasps of breath he said, "No, Beautiful, no!" and began to stagger backwards towards the doorway. "Let me go, Beautiful," he forced out. The kids began to shout "'Ray, ray,'" and jump up and down. "I can't see you," the technician forced out again in a series of loud gasps. "If I could I'd . . ." And the children screamed, "No, no, don't show! No, no, don't show!" Now the man was slammed up against the doors. He began to clutch his belly but also to spin in circles looking, then clutching at the empty air. "No, no, don't show!" the kids' scream continued. The technician stopped, knock-kneed, cramped, and his head began to move as if he was watching something spiral upward. "Go! Go!" the kids screamed. Finally the man's head was looking straight upward. His legs firmed up, his cramps left. He lifted his arms slowly and widened them and shouted, "No, no, don't go!" "Go! Go!" the kids screamed and began to dance up and down. With a great cry of despair, the technician hurled himself against the glass doors into the building. The doors gave and he reeled inside before the second doors like someone caught in a cell. The kids kept chanting, this time to him, "Go! Go! Go! Go!" He spun against the second set of doors and was gone. The kids were released. They turned to the next thing, which was hunger and one another and formed a crowd below a crowd of satisfied parents.

But the woman with her daughter was not satisfied. The girl was still deeply sad. So the woman moved through the crowd and up to the doors then through them into the reception space where a lot of the personnel had been gathered and looking out through the windows. And there was the technician drinking some water from a cup, unbuttoned to cool down from his exertions. The little girl recognised him. And she walked up under him as one does under the prow of a ship. He hunkered down on his heels. "Why did you kill and eat her?" the little girl asked. "I just pretended to," the man said. "Why did you pretend to?" the little girl asked. "So I could make you careful," the man said. "She's gone," the little girl said. "Oh," said the man, "what do I do now?" "You have to be good or she'll never come back," the little girl said. "You think I can?" the man asked. The little girl didn't know. "You have to not eat people," she said. "I promise," the man said, "from now on no people. But what if I get hungry?" "Peanut butter," the little girl said. "Will she come back then?" the man asked. The little girl shook her head no. "I have to tell her," she said. "Where is she?" the man asked. "It's a secret," the little girl said. "Is she in jail?" the man asked. The little girl shook her head no. "Ah," said the man, "she's in people. Right?" The little girl nodded yes. "If I eat people she goes. If I don't eat people she stays. Right?" The little girl nodded yes. "Okay, only peanut butter from now on."

The little girl turned and went back to her mother near the door and was ready to leave. The mother spoke to the man, "The next time this happens I sue you and the network for every last penny, do you understand?" "Remember, Lady," the man said, "only peanut butter."

Laugh Like a Donkey, Cry Like a Girl

*The Lord has given me a disciple's
tongue. . . Each morning he wakes
me to hear, to listen like a disciple.*
—Isaiah 50:4

"I'm a cold man, emotionally," a priest said to a woman sitting next to him on an El Al flight to Tel Aviv, "so I'm not really afraid." They had been talking since Rome, though she had a head set on, and were now over the Greek islands of the Aegean. They had been talking about threats to aircraft from terrorists and the woman had said she felt the danger almost every minute. "I go to the Holy Land often," the priest said, "because I get surprised into feeling something I could never feel on my own."

That puzzled the woman. She was in the window seat and could see the south coast of Turkey off in the distance. She pointed. "Nothing minor about Asia," she said. Then, "Would you tell me what you mean?"

"Well," the priest said, "one time I was there I discovered how contagious a donkey's laugh is. I was down near the Dung Gate to Jerusalem and this donkey lets go a laugh so ridiculous the whole of me was tickled and I started to shake and couldn't stop for hours. And I was seeing shepherds and sheep and mighty fortresses and valleys of judgment and I kept laughing like a helpless kid. Finally, up on Mt. Sion, I said this has got to stop. But I had to keep turning toward walls I was laughing so much. I stopped because I was exhausted, but also because I had absorbed something."

"You weren't laughing at the whole thing?" the woman asked.

"Maybe," the priest answered. "But within a few hours I was crying at the whole thing."

"How so?" the woman asked, her eyes roaming the south coast.

"I'm boring you," the priest said.

"No, you're surprising me," the woman said, "for someone who is cold, that was a warm reaction to a donkey."

"Next one has to do with a girl," the priest said, and he waited.

"I'd be more interested in a boy," she said.

"You have to take what you can get," the priest replied. "I get donkeys and camels and girls."

"Where'd the camel come from?" the woman asked.

"Oh," the priest said, "he was seated like a sphinx outside Gethsemane. He hissed. What a great hiss! His driver used him for photos. You could ride him like Lawrence of Arabia, or match profiles with him, for modest amounts of money. But he hissed regularly to show what he thought of it. And I often wish I could hiss like that."

"You're picking up weapons against religion," the woman said.

"Not really," the priest said, "unless girls are weapons against religion. I guess for some people they are!"

"You mean they steal priests?" the woman asked.

"Steal nothing," the priest said. "Get stolen maybe. I've seen a lot of cases."

"What about this one?" the woman said.

"Which one?" asked the priest.

"The one that goes with the donkey and the camel," she answered.

"Oh, yes," the priest said. "The evening of the day I couldn't stop laughing I was pretty empty inside, my usual self. So I go to a mass on Mt. Sinai, the Benedictine Abbey of the Dormition, great name. Anyway, it's supposed to be the real place of the Last Supper. Forty-five priests there. All scholars on a tour. And the Last Supper turned into the Honor of the Regiment it was so formal. Read. Move in half circle. Bow. Sing antiphon. Repeat. Repeat. By the time we left with candles I was longing for my friend the donkey. So down we go in a file with candles along the south wall of Jersualem. Mine got blown out in no time and I was glad, it was a distraction, I nearly stepped in a hole tending it. So we cross the Kedron and climb the road to Gethsemane, one of them anyway, the one with the church and the rock of agony, and I feel nothing, even inside the church, the rock bare in front of me, and people all around on their knees praying. So I went outside, I don't know why, and stood someplace along the fence enclosing the olive grove. Just outside that grove lived the hissing camel and his driver.

Well, the trees were in blossom and there were flowers out there in the dark also and up above, lighted by the paschal moon, the west wall of Jerusalem. I was alone I thought, but heard someone crying down the fence from me some ways to my left. I turned and I looked, it was a young woman, I said girl because I love that word, but nobody else does for anyone over 10, so a young woman. And I thought, 'My God, she's crossing two thousand years to connect with a man! Maybe Jesus should have been a woman for me and I could have done it!' That thought came later. But I went from empty to full in one second. Surprised. My eyes even got wet. So in one day I learned to laugh like a donkey, hiss like a camel, and cry like a girl. End of story."

"Gloomy," said the woman, and removed her earphones. She seemed to have been listening to them as well.

"I don't mind," the priest said, "gloomy is empty and empty is open and open is hungry."

"Ah," the woman said, "Then what if I gave you a surprise before you even get there?"

"I'd like that," the priest said.

"Maybe not," the woman said. "It's this. You are not going to see the Holy Land this trip. We are all going to be sequestered when we land. All checked out again. Then all put back on board and returned to Rome. The reason will be we cannot find the precise person on board whom we know is dangerous and being sent in to cause an incident. We had to come on from Rome because the checking could not really be done there."

The priest said nothing, just waited. The south coast of Turkey was farther off in the distance. And the plane was beginning its series of turns on command from ground control so ground could know nothing was sneaking in behind it. "I am a lawyer," the woman continued, "but also an agent for Intelligence. I'm sitting beside you because you were one of the suspects. Priest. Frequent flyer. There are Christian Palestinians in your parish. But you are not a suspect now. So my earphones tell me. There is nothing firm on the others either. So surprise! You are going back to Rome."

"That's not the surprise," the priest said, "though it is one, to be sure."

"No, I imagine not," the woman said, "the surprise is my saying this to you."

"Yes," he said. "I am that innocent."

"It's that you blush," the woman said.

"Monkey see no evil, monkey blush no evil?" the priest asked.

"Just so," the woman answered. "And I hope the only evil you see happened two thousand years ago. And you can only get there by donkey or camel or girl."

"I'm cold because no one wants me, Miss Lawyer," the priest said. "One has to kill to be wanted, pardon the pun."

"I want you, Mr. Priest," the woman said, "though you are dangerous if you have *learned* to blush. There are things only the innocent can see. Tell me one more surprise before we land. I would be grateful."

"Well, it would be about my Irish brogue," the priest said in a very quiet voice.

"Do you have one?" the woman asked.

"An Arab taxi driver thinks so," the priest replied.

Dumb Like a Fox

*Let us celebrate the feast, by getting
rid of the old yeast of evil and wicked-
ness, having only the unleavened bread
of sincerity and truth.*
                                    —1 Cor 5:8

"You're asking me did my husband commit suicide?" a woman said to a crowd of news people. They were in the foyer of a hospital. She was leaving. Her husband's body was back in emergency where she had just left it. He had been a hero in two wars, enough for two movies of spectacular exploits, then a star mountain climber, until he began to have strokes, then an author through dictation to her. "Yes, he did," she said to the media. "You're asking me did I help him?" she went on. "No, I didn't." She heard some more voices. "No one could ever stop him doing what he wanted to do," she said in one direction. "It was a cyanide capsule," she said in another. "He got it from an old kit he used in the service," she said in a third. "Behind the lines work. In Korea. When he went to find prison camps."

She got a little confused by the next barrage. "No, I never checked his things. I never thought this." She heard a follow up question. "Because I hoped he would never give up on life," she answered. She listened again. "Yes, he was very damaged. He could do very little for himself, or so I thought." She listened, then said, "He crawled. He tumbled himself out of the chair and crawled, or rather pushed himself along the floor. I think he then raised himself up an armchair using his teeth. Then he knocked the kit loose from the trophy shelf. He butted it with his head some way. I don't know how he opened it. It may have broken open when it fell. There was this snuffbox-like container. He bit it open I think. And it looks as if the pills were scattered, so he had to crawl some more and pick one up with his tongue. That's where I found him." She listened. Then said, "I was down in the laundry room. He used to insist on a lot of changes. He loved to be clean." Then, "Yes, all his life, even though he fought in dirt, or climbed on rock, he had to have clean clothes." Then, "No I will not miss him." "Will he have a hero's funeral? Are you asking me? I can't hear?" "Yes, he will, I am sure." "Why will I not miss him? You don't really want to know. I'm leaving now. I have to arrange."

She began to move through the media group towards the front door. She had arrived in an ambulance, so would have to hail a cab. A woman reporter spotted that so took her arm and said, "I'd be glad to run you home." "Please do," the other woman said, "I'm embarrassed to stand here." "Come," the reporter said. They went across the lot to her car, a neat Datsun two door sport. As the reporter pulled out she said, "Tell me which way." The woman did. After a few minutes on the road, the reporter asked, "Why won't you miss him, would you mind telling me?" "On or off the record?" the woman asked. "Whichever," the reporter said. "Okay, decide after," the woman said.

Then she went on, "I kept him alive after those wars. I had the three children and a husband who wanted to kill himself almost every minute. I detest death as a solution! My father killed himself when I was little and he ruined life all around him. So I married my hero thinking he would spit in death's eye. Instead he wanted to jump in and drown. I started then to find ways for him to risk death. I planned all those climbs for him, did all the research, got him alive to the dangers, set up the lectures that earned the money. And the house used to be seething with planning. The children thought eagerness to live was eating him up, but it was eagerness to die. Yet he succeeded every time. So I managed to switch his effect on me and on the children. They are out there now chewing great chunks out of life. And I have learned to spit. When the strokes came, he pleaded with me to kill him. He turned me into a sentencing judge. That's when I found the writing ploy."

"I had him mumble to me day in and day out, had him wrack his memory for details, then I pieced it all together. I would read it back to him and it would move him for a while. Then lose its effect. The last few years I could think of nothing, and I saw death gain on me in him. I did not know about those pills. And I forgot what ferocious willpower he had when he wanted. So there, young woman, I will not miss him, he defeated me, and maybe he damaged the children. I have to phone them. He'll be a further hero. And I'll get the flag in my lap from two impeccable marines." She stopped speaking.

"Why should you want him to go on living?" the reporter asked, almost meekly, as if to say it is better to go out when broken than to stay behind and live like a thing. "Because he knew what I was doing!" The woman answered. She said it tautly. "He thought I had something else up my sleeve." She said this even more tautly. "Thought I was starting to bring in religion. Suffer for the sins of the world kind of stuff. Oh!" The woman expelled a breath. "It was the opposite. I started to read him creation stories. Everything wasn't broken. Everything wasn't meant to be broken. I wanted the opposite effect! But he wanted that damned darkness where things disappear. I had to put flowers out of reach, where he couldn't knock them over. He would not let anything rise!"

The woman reporter was embarrassed now. She said, again almost meekly, "You might be different if you were as bad off as he." "I might be different, yes," the woman said, "but if you were, I'd be doubly damned. Do you see? Whoever is alive and whole has to keep faith. Have you ever seen someone in perfect health who wants to die? Can you feel the contradiction?" She was looking at the woman reporter now. "So when I am broken, do you walk through the door and say let me help you with this little cyanide? Or do you come in and whether it's a lie or not try to make sense? I wanted to convince him that life is to be reborn. I could read stories about it from now to Doomsday. I did not detest his broken body. He did." She was quiet after saying this. Then, "So the undertaker will straighten him out, put him as a colonel asleep in a box with his congressional medal and purple hearts and oak leaf clusters. Ready for resurrection into the eternal Marine Corps. And somebody will read 'The Lord is my Shepherd.' Damn! Too late! It should be done beforehand. So the corpse can see how dumb we are or how desperate we are!"

"You are not dumb," the reporter said. "Maybe I am," the woman said. "I've known for a long time he was my father, not my man, and I was trying to undo a death. That's double dumb." "Like a fox," the reporter said. "I need more directions." "Next off ramp," the woman said, "then down two miles to the water. We're on a tidal creek. It's been a joy to me." "Was it for him?" the reporter asked. "When the tide was out, yes," the woman answered, "when it was down to mud and shells."

2nd Sunday, Easter

One Man's Loss . . .

You believe because you can see me.
Happy are those who have not seen
and yet believe.
—John 20:29

"Okay, what about me?" a man said to the water. He was standing at the edge of the tide. There was a small surf running, but not enough to take the sand out from under him. To his left and right was the beach, a half mile either way, houses behind him, a poor folks' place. He laughed at that, you still needed cash. The sea had been God to him for a long time, he could talk to it, it talked back and made sense. He was ready to walk into it for good. His wife was gone, buried a month ago, and the small cottage was senseless, not sad, just senseless.

"Here I come," he said. But it was cold water, April water. However warm the sun was, and however soft the breeze, it would take weeks to warm this thing. And the man's ankles were numb. "You'd bite me," he said. So he backed a bit to where the wet sand was bearable. The tide kept coming, pushing the man back a few inches at a time. He was smiling. "A nice no," he said. "When you warm, I'm coming."

A shadow and a whistle of feathers went by him, a big gull across the wind. "Wrong place, buddy," the man said, "little pickings here. Go inland. Big dumps." But it was a fine flyer, not spectacular as the wild swans who really pumped by you overhead going some place important. The gull dropped just yards away. "Ugly bugger," the man thought as it waddled a bit. "You watch for someone else to catch something, then you go rob. Cormorants are smart. They eat before they surface." He turned back toward the sea. "Really, I'm a scavenger now, let me out of this." He started again into the water but it was colder if anything. The wind was off-

68

shore. It was pushing the warm surface out, baring the cold beneath. So he backed again. There was a seal's head showing out a hundrd yards. "Something running," the man thought. "In Abraham's bosom. Where she is, I hope."

"Ah," he said, and he walked along the edge of the tide, "you killed this beach once. I remember you. The wildest thing. Up over my head and raking this sand out like madness, right down to the gravel and dirt. You laid it out like an undertaker at a famine. And then you fattened it up again, smooth like hands over skin, I never saw anything so sly, night and day, like someone rubbing wood to a polish. You could come at me again if you don't take me first." He stopped and looked out. "My grandmother buried two old sons. I remember she stooped into the grave of the last one, we thought she'd fall, and his sons were so grown and weary of him that they were glad of her grief or their father would have gone in cold. And I can be gotten to again. And I'd rather not."

At this end of the beach where it was flatter the waves had a nice long run, breaking like smiles of pleasure, and the man noticed. "You're happy at something. What is it?" he asked. "You think I'm morose?" He turned and started the other way along the tide's edge. "You haven't got it yet," he then said. "You keep splashing me. And throwing gulls at me. And sounds like a baby sucking. And all this blue green. It's so much less than she." There were some sandpipers ran ahead of him, piercing the sand with their pipes and coming up with things. "I've no one to feed," he said, looking square at the sea now. "That's it. Like the baby's gone and I have the milk drying inside me. And the blood stopping its month. And the moisture going. And you're still like a clambake saying come on its fun." He started again. "But you're good, you're consoling me so the time will pass and I'll forget." He went on some yards, then said, "She didn't know her name, never mind yours, she couldn't finish a prayer with an amen even. You remember? I said to you that day we had both lost her, and you'd better be ready to make no sense when she came, be ready to live with that blank look, unless you had a mind in your two hands with everything in it she was. Or she'd slip between your fingers like this sand on a hot summer."

He turned again, out to sea. "There's not nothing, is there?" he asked. "If you lost your food, say, or you lost your rhythm, who would come?

I've been at another edge, up around the moon, through a capsule window, and there is nothing beyond the rims, a black eternity, if you want it you can have it!" The surf was a little rougher now that the beach was steeper. And the sand was drawn some out from under the man's feet. "Perfect," the man said, feeling the tickle. He stood and let himself sink deeper. It was hard to balance so he had to step free, and watch the two holes fill. "You've always got an answer," he said. "You keep me moving. Even the summer I tried to sit here after my job was finished. You kept itching at me. Until I was in swimming most of the time and I looked like finnan haddie."

He was nearly at the other end of the beach now. A stream cut right across, cold fresh water from some ponds back behind, busy, busy, running into the surf with a wrestle, it was a nice churning. "I could do it this way," the man said. Then, "No, I couldn't, I'd float up dead, too big for the gulls, and there'd be a scene and people afraid and bruised in their spirits. That's what you mean, isn't it? A crab is different." He crossed the stream, it was strong and the bottom gravelly so he had to do some cavorting to make it. The sand on the other side was harder packed for some reason and led to a rock promontory with a lobster shed and eatery on top. "You run out here," the man said, "you disappear around the bend where I can't chase you."

A dog came swinging around him, from someone, a woman up on the sea wall with a leash in her hand. "I won't tell a soul," said the man to the dog who should have been on the leash. "Just don't crap here," he went on, "ruins the picnic." The woman waved. He waved back. "If I forget you," the man said, "may my tongue dry and my hand wither." He stopped at the end of the beach where the rocks rose. "She forgot you," he said to the sea. And he began to walk into it again, but again it froze his ankles and forced him back on the warmer sand. "You're obstinate," he said. His footprints had been wiped out all the way back along the beach. "It's all new," the man said, "I've never been here." And he started back.

Listen Groucho

Did not our hearts burn within us . . .
—Luke 24:32

"My father didn't want to die," a woman said. It was to a group counselling session, and she was depressed because her father had died.

"He liked things. But when he knew he'd have to go he said to me, 'You take a pill, no sense in you staying here.' 'Why not?' I said. 'I'm still young, I'm rich, I can do things.' 'You're ugly,' he said, 'you've got my nose and your mother's chin and we'll be gone and you won't be able to explain.' He thought he was funny so he laughed and his heart nearly stopped right then. 'You bring out the worst in me,' he said. 'I should have been a comedian and left your mother alone.' So I said, 'I get all your money. I go to a hospital. They take half my nose and put it in my chin and there! I am Greta Garbo.' 'Who says you get all my money?' he said and I said, 'I says, and every judge'll agree.' 'Well, you can keep it,' he says, 'won't do you any good either.' 'Listen Groucho,' I said, 'you did the smoking, not me, that's why you're a hiss like a kettle. I told you, I told you, and I had to smoke what you smoked including the stupid cigars.' 'They helped me think,' he said, 'that's where your money comes from.' 'It comes from me,' I said, 'I spotted most of your deals. You just happened to have the pocket.' 'I don't want to go,' he said, 'it's empty dead.' 'You don't know,' I said. 'Maybe you get new lungs and a fresh cigar.' 'You're cooking me here,' he said, 'like a wienie on a stick. You're cruel.' 'Geez I'm not,' I said to him, 'you wanted me to croak myself so I wouldn't have what you didn't have. I'm just protecting myself.' Then he got very sad, first time I ever saw sad win out, he had a deal he was watching every minute. 'What's life without me?' he said and he wanted me to say *nothing* because we did everything together. He wasn't kidding when he said I was ugly. Cyrano de Bergerac's sister. I can see you see." The woman said this to the group.

"So he made up for everything, he thought, by teaching me to fly his plane and deal his stocks and break men's clubs and country clubs. I could hit a golf ball a mile and nearly turned pro except then he was bouncing around the middle east learning what was up and had me along so I could pick up Arabic. I can pick up languages. And nobody thought I was a woman until up close, but they could smell his money so they treated me kindly. Or he would have cut them cold. And I went along with all this because I could forget and really use myself instead of turning into an ash-can someplace for whatever I could pick up on my own. He knew I was tempted to die with him. Out easy for me after he came to a halt like a steam locomotive. And I think that broke something in him, not something good, something bad, like a mirror gets broken for Narcissus or somebody drains the pond and says look at me and I'll tell you what you look like. 'Okay,' he said, 'but a nose job won't do it.' 'Aw come on,' I said. 'I stopped looking a long time ago. I go to the zoo. They love me.' 'Okay,' he said, 'but they'll be after your money.' 'Let 'em,' I said. 'I'll tell them when they wake up in the morning I'll be beautiful and they'll be glad they took an awful chance.' He started to cry. 'Don't feel sorry for yourself,' I said, '*you* won't even believe it!' And he looked hurt at that so I knew he wasn't feeling for himself. He loved me."

The woman stopped. Then said to the group, "And you're supposed to interrupt when you don't understand and can do me some good with what you know." But the group said nothing.

"He loved me so much he couldn't admit it. I don't mean queer love. How he ever made it with my mother I'll never know. And she didn't either, which is why she left and went back to the old country and found somebody else. Boy, girl, it didn't matter, I just caught everything quickly, traipsed around behind him like a duck and when I started to menstruate he got a book himself and read it to me, gave me the book and said, 'Look up what happens from now on, we have other things to do.' But here he was sitting and I knew what he didn't want to leave and he saw that I had spotted it and he had to find a way now to make me stay because he knew I was horsing around. You understand? There's such a big hole in my life, it's filled with cash, but the cash is like leaves under a tree and there's a wind. Everybody else is dull. I'm dull. It's just stocks and bonds with dull people and not with a man who made all the monkeys in the trees chatter. So he said to me, 'Don't take that pill. I want to be alone. I'm tired of you hanging around. I'll go over on the other side and marry an oriental who has no nose. Worse that can happen is that mine'll come out half size. Still big but not a rudder.' 'So what's with this alone?' I said. And he looked for something else. 'I have to be independent,' he said. 'She won't speak English. But I've got too much talent to keep to myself.' And he was looking at me and I saw that death look come up and he said straight out, 'Let me go alone, if you come I'd be double dead.' It was the alone that was choking him, not the bad lungs. 'There are people there,' I said. I don't know why. 'The opposite of here,' I said. 'You'll be me. I'll be you. Think you can take it?' I shouldn't have said that. I really loved what I am. And that's what I didn't get across to him. We had joked about it too long. And he went out on that. I have no way left. He just stopped breathing." The woman stopped talking. Then said, "So I love life and it's empty."

There was a rustle in the group, legs uncrossed, recrossed, some pulling at skirts and trousers. But no response. "When you're outside a nose like mine, outside a little chin, I suppose you feel uneasy. When you're inside its snap, crackle and pop if you let it, and things outside go. Like I'm going to be the last one in the world and I have to turn off the light." The woman looked around at the group. "So what's new?" she said. "You are," they said.

4th Sunday, Easter

Pit Stop Priest

My dear people, we are already the
children of God, but what we are to
be in the future has not yet been
revealed.
—1 John 3:2

"I'm like a pawn," a priest was saying, "I don't know it until later. Like the time they stole the hearse from in front of the church." He was talking to a young woman, college student, researching poor parishes, inner city, for Sociology 323. She looked puzzled. "Well, why steal a hearse?" the priest went on. They were in the pews of the church. The priest kept it open during the day, so that meant patrolling it, the sexton was out for lunch, so the priest was covering. "I lead the coffin down the aisle to the door, turn and pray it goodbye, an old parishioner with just friends for mourners, and I'm paying a good part of the bill, the city will give you a pauper's burial and it's not much. So I open the front door and no hearse. It was an old Cadillac to start with, the leasing companies never let the undertakers here have anything good, and its gone, the few flowers with it, and the undertaker says 'Shit' louder than any 'Amen.' I know there's something up. I tell everybody to wait, I go back in the Rectory, call the Police and tell them its more than swiping an old Cadillac hearse, maybe somebody wants to get rid of a body over in the Jersey dumps, I don't know. And bring a van, I tell them, I have a body to bury. So I take the parishioner to the grave in a police van. Meantime the Cadillac hearse goes to the airport, we find out later, picks up a body shipped back from overseas, all the papers right, delivers the body someplace and then gets parked neatly under a bridge for us to find two days later. Well, it was a lead coffin it probably picked up, but also probably loaded with cocaine. And that's just one instance of me doing one thing and somebody hiding behind me to do another. One time I kept losing that little St. Anthony statue over there. Then someone would mail me a new one right from Italy. Twice before I smartened up. Drugs are coming through this place like God unless I shut it up and throw away the key. The cops have had me checked with the bishop to see if I'm not some plant. They open every coffin that comes in here now. That extra body thing. With the undertaker tipped off to put some muscle in the pall bearers so they make it look like an easy job, little old lady."

"Why *not* lock it?" the young woman asked.

"Well," the priest said, "there's some black comedy to it, never a dull moment. I'm sitting here one day when I see a *guy* come out of the back confessional, you see the confessional down there under the choir loft? The door, two curtains to either side?"

"Yes," the young woman said.

"I'm the only one to hear confessions," the priest said. "Then a *woman* comes out of the same confessional, same side."

"That doesn't sound very funny," the young woman said.

"Well, when you are in those boxes," the priest said, "a red light goes on over the curtain and it says someone is inside. They're automatic in case the priest forgets to flick the switch. Red light, you get it?"

"Are you angered?" the young woman asked.

"No," the priest said, "no, if I could reduce all sins to fornication I'd do it. They didn't make a noise."

"You sound very beaten to me," the young woman said. "I know that's not the right thing to say. Maybe I'm asking you again why you don't lock the church and go somewhere more, more spiritual."

"O, you can't want a sermon from me," the priest said, "and you can't want a theory of praxis. Here I am, I'm sixty and someone comes in, sees me in the pew, I spend a lot of time here, comes up and sits and its someone whose lover has AIDS and he gave it to him. Well, he drops through the bottom of reality and I do too, I just drop with him, and we sit here like two guys in a waiting room and there's no train coming or going. Then he kisses me to see if I flinch and I don't, so he rubs his hand on the kiss and says Judas is gone. Was never here, I say. And he leaves breathing, I mean he wasn't when he came in. So that's one reason. And I know he won't leave his lover to the rats. I don't know how it works, I never did. You just be. I've had killers sit right where you are, cold, cold, geez, and I know they know they're lost and want nothing said. An hour once. He said 'I can't stop. So I stop myself.' And he put a hand up so I wouldn't say anything. And I knew he was saying the lesser of two evils. I know he didn't think that before he came in."

"Did he kill himself?" the young woman asked.

"Yes," the priest answered, "I read it in the paper. I knew. But then someone comes in who's so good you can't believe you're in the same world, or the someone has got to be a fake. A guy had memorized all of Dylan Thomas, I can hardly read Thomas on a page. An old teacher, you know, small pension, from public schools, but he goes around to the elderly reciting poems, not Thomas, he saves that for me because I'm smart, but old ballads, the lyrics of old tin pan alley tunes, sometimes hymn verses because the man can't sing. Then he does errands, gets prescriptions filled. I had to check him out on that, could be another trick for drugs, but he checked. He just loves beauty and he loves to share it, and old people don't mind, anything for company."

"What sustains you?" the young woman asked. "You don't seem to have any programs or any linkage to sister parishes, or any city or federal funds."

"You *do* want a sermon," the priest said.

"What can I write?" she asked. "It's fascinating to hear you about what goes on in the church, but I can't just tell stories, I'd flunk the course. I know you're doing me a favor."

"But it may not be one after all?" the priest asked.

"Right," the young woman said.

"Well, someone like me," the priest said, "becomes a center. I used the word pawn too. People play off a center for positive or negative reasons. I have no profit to gain. So I don't need to be shot. I have no tongue after someone talks to me. What's said is secret. So people can actually work through their worst selves with me, or strengthen their best, and I need say very little. But by the same token I can be used, I gave you the funeral example. And the open church example. And I'm like an ancient memory, that killer remembered some old form that went with his childhood. So sociologically speaking, I'm a lightning rod or a divining rod. Translate that into some appropriate jargon, okay?"

"Well, yes," the young woman said, "there are some categories, therapeutic ones, they are a bit cold, maybe like your killer, but they'll do." She was writing quickly as she spoke.

"So what about you?" the priest asked. "What are you in this for? You want to be a social worker?"

"No," she said.

The priest then said nothing more. He seemed to be thinking his own thoughts, about things that happened. His hand was on the pew in front of him and he was turned half sideways toward the young woman. Then he sat back and great peace seemed to come over him.

She said, "I'm making up for a life I took."

Beirut Concerto

My children, our love is not to be
just words or mere talk, but some-
thing real and active; only by this
can we be certain that we are the
children of the truth . . .
　　　—1 John 3:18-9

"Maybe you won't believe this," a woman was saying, "but I recover in a small cloister near the hospital. There are pointed arches, there is a fountain dripping when the water is on in the city, and moss, and someone, a monk, puts the goldfish back, from a jar, I've seen him. He lets me in, though he shouldn't. One of the monks was hit by shellfire and brought to the hospital. I'm the first doctor to see anyone. I make the decisions if we can save or not. The "nots" we put in the corridor with the families so they die with their own. But I saw we could save the monk. I made checkup visits later. So this one lets me in the cloister now for a few hours and they all know and leave it to me. He takes the goldfish back out when I leave and shuts the water off though he keeps the moss moist with some wet towels. And he rings a bell every fifteen minutes, a wonderful sweet bell, I don't know where he got it, he has a felt tipped hammer, so he reminds me of the time. I get only a few hours free on easy days. Bad days none at all.

Why am I telling you all this? Because you asked me what keeps me alive and I have no big answer like faith or love. I have neither. My husband died by a car bomb. He was buying a cake for his mother's birthday. And religion is firing these guns. Oh yes! *You* think not, *you* think power or territory, but it's religion because no one feels guilty. Except me. Every time I say 'this one has no chance, take him, take her to the corridor,' I feel guilty. But when I go into that cloister I do not feel so anymore. Though don't you think I should? It's like running away.

There was a bird the monk put in there last week, a songbird in a cage, and he put it in an angle of the cloister that acted like a megaphone and I was suspended listening to it. Even the crumps of those hideous shells couldn't quiet its singing. It was a concerto of real life. There was a bubble of joy in me. If I moved it would go out my head or my toes. Then the bell. He struck it twice for each hour as on a ship, and once for the quarter. It was twelve forty-five. The bird tried to match the note with its own voice as if fighting for supremacy, and the bird did find the harmonic, then sang so much against that bell that it was with it like something eternal. The bird got confused when the bell stopped and searched with its voice for some other conflict but could find none. I tried to whistle and all I did was wheeze. So it was reduced to spurts of singing to itself. Which was beautiful also. Then came the single stroke of one. And the bird and I stopped everything. Even as the crump of shells went on I could hear the true silence.

Then the water in the fountain stopped, the power was cut again somewhere. The monk came out with his little plastic bag on a pole and caught the goldfish and put them in a large stoneware jar. He gave me a nod and I could see he loved me as I sat there in my slacks and white coat with the blood spots on it. Loved me as he did the bird, the song, the strokes of the bell, the fish, the dripping water. I have found flowers on the bench where I sit on some days. They are from the chapel, I know it, he plucks a few from the vases. He is afraid of me too, the way monks are afraid of women, but this fear has turned into something lovely, it is a fear *for* me, as if to say there will be a hole in the world if I go, if the bird, the flowers, the bell go, and into that hole the real satan will come.

One day I was so tired I sat on another bench, in the sun, and leaned back against a pillar. And I fell asleep. I woke up to a rosewater scent. There was a light, light veil over my head, enough to keep the sun from burning me and yet let the heat through. It was a tabernacle veil and the monks might beat him if they knew. So I took it off. And I started to weep. I mean the tears just came. He must have been watching me and thought he had done something wrong because he came out from under a pillar and made a cross on himself, the kind we use to ask forgiveness. So

I held the veil to myself in my arms, and he knew and backed away. I could see how arthritic he was. Probably just suffered it for the world. I could hardly leave that day. But the shellfire intensified and the scream of the ambulances so I had to run out the door. I have never seen the damage to the human body as great as I saw then. Some new shell was being used, it blew up before it hit and filled the air with shrapnel. It was a week before I did anything but sleep, eat, and sew bodies back together. When I returned to the cloister I had every intention of dying. It was like a last visit to a daydream. I don't mean dying by my own hand. I mean just stopping. I think people can just stop. It's only a matter of time then. I rang the buzzer with my two longs and a short and the door clicked so I went in and sat where I usually do, but my head was down. It was too heavy to hold. I actually bent down to my own knees. I heard his old arthritic shuffle. And he did something monks never do. He began to move his hands back and forth across my shoulder blades. He sang a lullaby I recognised. An ancient one from up in the hills, one my grandmother had used but I hadn't heard since. So I straightened up, maybe just to breathe, and he shifted his hands to my head and simply stroked my hair, but no song now, he was a man, an old one, and he was touching a woman, not for anything but that she was a woman and grief could be stroked away. Then he put his hands again on my two shoulders and I leaned back into this thick wool robe, as I had into the pillar that day, and he said one thing to me I had not heard also for a long time, from the Song of Songs: "Love is stronger than death." But he almost said it as a question, his voice rising slightly at the end.

And there it all was before me. Was his love for me strong enough to keep me from death? Was mine strong enough to keep him or anyone else from death? Was this cloister strong enough, its sights, its sounds? And somehow I knew the other monks were watching him and for changed reasons, they could smell the death coming over the wall with every wisp of smoke. I saw that life depended on my soul as much as on my brains and my skill. He sensed I knew with his hands. He backed away from me. I could hear his bones creak as he moved. And the monastery seemed to let out a breath. And to breathe. So here, I've told you.

The cloister is damaged a bit now. One side took a shell that left it rubble. But he is in there moving piece after piece out of the central courtyard, uncovering the grass. It is pitiful to watch and his heart won't take it long. He is neglecting me, he knows it, while I am sitting. But the bird is somewhere, and there is a clear plastic sack in the shade where I can see it, it has water and three goldfish. But when I leave I turn back. He is looking at me, holding a stone or trying to straighten his stiff spine. And he is weeping. Weeping that he cannot have something beautiful for me. He doesn't know.

6th Sunday, Easter

Nun Goes Native

Everyone who loves is begotten by God
and knows God, because God is love.
—1 John 4:7

"You had a great aunt in that order," a man was saying. He and his daughter were looking at a school catalogue, at the smaller colleges where some family sense of life could be kept. "I mean I had, she'd be your great, great. I never told you?" "No," the daughter said. "Your family's too big. We haven't even done the first cousins." They were comfortable with each other, man and daughter. This part of the family was not big. Just two in fact. His wife had died in a car accident. Hit by a drunk driver. When the girl was small. He had not remarried because his memories were still strong and nourishing. And his daughter had had eye problems from the same accident. So he had spent great amounts of time reading to her throughout school while surgery was correcting her sight. Which was fine now. And he was an insurance broker, which could also gobble time.

"Well, this aunt worked with the Indians, if I remember. I met an old nun at the funeral who just grabbed me and had to tell me everything, I'll never forget it, that wake in the parlor of the convent, and I was really your age, but this nun was about ready to burst wrapped up in that crazy dress they had, here, like this one on the foundress of the school, like someone peeping out of a baby's bassinet, how did they hear anything? Funny, but I think the nun who grabbed me loved my aunt, I mean really loved her, but couldn't say it to anybody, not even my aunt, but here she was dead, and family all looked so square, and I'm there all apple cheeked and round and maybe understanding. She'd never get another chance."

"You're never going to tell me," the daughter said.

82

"Your aunt," he said, "out with the Indians, decided to go Indian. First by hanging beads on her habit, then by wearing belts. But she saw that was fake. So she got Indian dress. And one day she walked into class, out of the habit, in Indian dress, and there was an uproar. The Indian girls loved it. The nuns hated it. So they ordered her out of the reservation and she refused to go. She wore a habit in the convent, she wore Indian garb in the schoolroom. And she had her pupils teach her Indian, they were Potawatomy, I think. And by a cute trick, she taught them the grammar they needed to explain to her their own language. This old nun kept stopping the story to tell me how beautiful she looked when she let her hair grow back and made a braid of it and wore a headband. Well, the other nuns actually tried to be physical with her but she was too strong. She insisted they all go Indian, this convent schooling for Indian girls was a farce.

The Indian men took it as a joke. She actually did a Lady Godiva on them, one of those festival days. She got a paint and rode it naked right through town so they could all see she was a woman if she wanted to be, any way she wanted to be. The bishop ordered her out of the territory. But she refused to go again. He was saying Mass one day, a confirmation, in one of those old wooden churches, and she appeared out of the sacristy at the offertory and started to dance an Indian dance, the one for before the hunt to give the hunter strength. The two chaplains grabbed her. But she wrestled free. And that became part of the dance.

Oh! She was beautiful, the old nun kept saying. And saying she was right to do what she did. And they hated her. They drove her away. Put her in a truck while two of them sat on her all the way to St. Louis. And the old nun said, 'She kept stroking my thigh all the way, as if she knew what I felt and she was mocking me. But she wasn't. She was telling me that love needs courage.'"

"You sure that nun wasn't off?" the daughter asked.

"What do I know?" the father answered. "I know that's what they do now, the nuns, if they teach Indians. Especially up in Canada."

"So they kept her in St. Louis?" the daughter asked.

"Yes," he answered, "and apparently she began a campaign against the Bureau of Indian Affairs. She wrote to all the reservations, got testimonies, proposed solutions. Plus she was teaching college. And wouldn't she every now and then do an Indian dance! Though in her habit, not Indian dress."

"Why didn't she just leave that bunch?" the daughter asked. "Get out there on her own. Start a school back on the reservation."

"Women were tied then," the father said. "They had to make do often with what they were in. The Bureau would have thrown her out if the Order hadn't. Most women didn't just land on their feet in those days. She was something, though. It wasn't just the old nun that was choked up that night. Some of the others were really discomposed."

"What did the old nun do, just let you go then?" the daughter asked.

"Well no, now that you ask," the father answered. "She shoved something in my pocket and asked me to keep it in the family. It would get thrown away in the Order. And I couldn't look at it until later because she was holding me as if to keep from falling apart. And all this at the back of the parlor in the convent and in somewhat of a whisper. I didn't think of my pocket until later when my hands were cold outside. So I pull out this Indian headband. And I put it back in. Dumped it in my drawer later. And I think I still have it somewhere."

The father and daughter were looking at one another and both thinking the same question. "That old nun," the father said, "I bet she did it, she's the one who enforced the discipline, I bet she was the watchdog who loved what she watched. Ohhh geez!"

"So she'd have access to the headband," the daughter said.

"Right," the father said.

"You think your aunt was gay?" the daughter asked.

"No," the father said, "but I think she loved everything intensely, the cowboys *and* the indians."

"Then the old nun?" the daughter asked.

"Yes," the father said. "But not until the night of the funeral could she admit it. And I don't know it until right now."

"Could you give me that headband?" the daughter asked.

"Wait a bit," the father said, "let me find out what it is first, I mean what kind, and maybe why she wore it and not something else. And I want to check back on this old nun. Because maybe the band belongs in the grave if it doesn't make something happen to me."

"You sound superstitious," the daughter said, and she started to laugh a bit.

"Well, look at it this way," the father said. "That band opened somebody up and closed somebody down. That old nun wanted to open me up. I think she felt damned. Unless I did something. She may be hanging in space somewhere to see which way I go."

"Oh," the daughter said, and she grabbed him, "you put anybody in hell and they'll love it."

"Like my aunt, you mean?" the father asked.

"You're scary, Pop," the daughter said.

"Then we go to another school," he said.

"No, this one," she said.

He raised his eyebrows. "Scary who?" he asked.

7th Sunday, Easter

Kiss and Tell

No one has ever seen God;
but as long as we love one another
God will live in us . . .
—1 John 4:12

"You ask me how one keeps a tradition going?" a man said. He was a priest at a conference on vocations. One of a panel. And he had been asked the question. "Maybe by painting a rosy picture." He paused to reflect. "Sometimes at night when I can't sleep I seem to be in a planetarium and there's a row of buttons in front of me. I push one and the star it controls gets brighter so I can see where it is among all the others. Well, it isn't really any fun because the process raises exactly the question how did any of us get through? Why do I represent a tradition now? The buttons are really names I press, names to see where we were."

"I remember one guy in the early years who used to go into a closet off the small study hall where we were working away. We'd hear the sounds of horses' hooves, we'd hear neighing, for about five minutes, then he'd come out, break silence and say, 'Have to feed 'em.' And we'd burst. He left. And there was a man with a huge baby-like head who thought what was wanted was study and prayer so that's all he did. Until his head cracked. I mean ached so he couldn't use it. Lovely, gentle guy who disappeared very quietly. Authorities never let us see anyone go. Then there was a guy with a glorious deep voice who could pronounce Latin and English perfectly. It took years for him to crack. But his voice stayed beautiful. Oh, I know I should talk about the strong ones, a guy named Nails, and that's what he was in later years, someone able to live under gunfire and stay analytic. But there was another tough guy who was really hiding a gentle self that just wanted to sing, not do penance for the sins of the world. I have felt sometimes that the Holy Spirit really doesn't know who will make it. Like nature with its dandelion seeds, millions on the wind to have a few take root. We certainly didn't know if we were going to make it, though some did know. An interesting type who decided early we were being fed a lot of bullshit and that the vocation was bigger than the system that nurtured it."

"So my answer is you keep a tradition going at great risk to body and soul. If a price has to be paid, you have to pay it. But what you buy must be worth it. That's not the rosy picture approach and maybe I just lost you."

He finished speaking and pushed the microphone back from him a bit so the next question could rise from the floor of the auditorium to any of the panel, or any of the panel could redo his answer to the previous one. He was back inside his planetarium again, the names, the people, so he didn't notice that the next question was also directed to him. But he felt people looking. So he brought the microphone closer again and said, "I'm sorry. My head filled up with names, just after I spoke, I didn't hear the question."

A voice spoke again, "What would be your rosy picture?"

"Oh," he answered, "you say to someone if you have a vocation, it's within you and from God. You cannot betray yourself if you follow it. You will bring charity into the life of the world every day you live that vocation. And God will be loved for the love God has given. You will be at the source of life every minute." He stopped and pushed the microphone back, leaving the question for others to comment on.

But the same voice from the audience spoke again, "Well, why are you afraid to give that message?"

The priest pulled the microphone more slowly back to himself. "Because I've seen God destroy too many people," he said. There was a gasp in the crowd. "Look," he said, "any love will find your weakness and break you there. I remember Gabriela Mistral's poem about the rose where she says do not trifle with the rose, she will sear you with her flame. And she has another one about a pot just out of the kiln, white and dry, she describes it as love hot with thirst. I think God doesn't know how attractive such love is and how it fractures us in a second. You have to grow people to a certain size. I'm not talking playing God. I'm talking playing human. Fanatics you can have quickly. You just lobotomize them with God-wills-it. Anything that happens earns paradise. But people who can approach a very strong love? And not be overwhelmed? Or broken as most often happens? You have to have signals so human that people know they can't fall below a certain point. That underneath them is God as well as above them. But even that's not right. The risk is gone. We have to know that God is as much at risk as we. That God can disappear for the same reasons we do. Though I remember Dylan Thomas's borrowing of scripture, 'And death shall have no dominion!' It's just that there has to be a fragility to God or we are the only ones who bear the consequences of the rosy picture. And please don't say the Cross to me. We're in a century that makes the Cross look pale. In fact, we can't keep it unless we close our eyes. So nurturing a human being is absolutely essential, in my view. And I think that human being builds up a taste for love, a wise palate, or better a wise touch, so when it is mature it can lay a love on God which is mature, the way a man or a woman can put a hand on you to catch your attention."

"You're a humanist," a voice said up from the audience.

"No, I'm not," the priest shot back. "I'm saying when the love of God approaches you, you better be ready or you'll break, sooner or later. It's the tradition of love we're talking about continuing. But suppose that love has left a trail of wreckage? *Then* people become humanists, they never blame God, they say the human couldn't hack it. One day I was in my room studying theology and this whirlwind of a guy came in. We had watched him devour knowlege magnificently for ten years, whapping back and forth from his room to the library, he hardly slept. He asked me that day was I the judge who the day before had condemned him in criminal court? Then he said something further, 'I can't distinguish between dreams and reality.' I said no. He left the room. Left the seminary for a hospital where he spent years struggling with schizophrenia. Ten more years pass and I read his death notice in the paper. I'm sure he killed himself. We should have begged him on bended knee to be human. But for us it was like watching fireworks. Like having a superstar to flatter our own efforts. That whole system was not intent on producing love. It was intent on producing fireworks, superstars. Oh!" The priest pushed the microphone away as if for a final time.

But the voice came again, "You seem to be getting even with God. Could that be so?"

"It could be," the priest said. "Or I could be clarifying what that love is. I have a friend who thinks the Grand Canyon is God. We stood on the south rim one evening looking at sunset colors shifting, changing, down 5,000 feet to the river. I said to him, 'This place is telling us something. If you know me, I will kiss you. If you do not know me, I will kill you.' That place is a desert. You never go alone. You never go without rules. The very next day, when we were on the bottom, we heard about a guy who went off by himself climbing. He fell and killed himself. And his pack was in the camp two days before someone spotted it. So a ranger who could almost read tracks on stone went out looking and found him. The experience of that canyon was fantastic for me. But it still says the same thing, 'If you know me, I will kiss you. If you do not know me, I will kill you.' And my friend still thinks the canyon is God."

The Meat Approach

You take back your spirit, they die,
returning to the dust from which they came.
You send forth your spirit, they are created,
and you renew the face of the earth.
　　　　　—Psalm 104: 29-30

A woman was dodging rocks. Her press colleagues had told her not to get caught between the throwers and the military. But she had to find an angle to find news. There was just survival right now, and safety in a doorway a few feet off. She slammed into it as a rock grazed her thigh, tore her skirt a bit. She could look from here.

First thing she saw was someone take a rubber bullet in the head, snapped the young kid around and dropped him. The others ran leaving him. He tried to struggle to his feet, but a second shot caught him. A few other shots screeched off the street near. The woman ran towards him with her arms raised and her camera tossing on her chest and when she reached him she got down on all fours facing the military. The boy was jerking on the ground underneath her. A stone hit her on the buttocks and bit into her, so she swung around and held up both hands to stop, but they didn't, the stones seemed to come in faster, she bent left and right to dodge some. Then the hurling stopped and the hurlers started to run away further. She heard the military pounding up behind her. She felt herself jerked to her feet, spun around, and shoved in the direction of the several jeeps blocking the road a hundred yards back. So she stumbled that way as two soldiers had the boy's legs and arms and were carrying him in the same direction.

The rocks started to sail in again so she twisted to look and up on the roof nearby were some throwers. She took another one on the shoulder which nearly broke it. If it had hit her head . . . There were shots and she saw some bodies spin backwards and disappear. She got back to the jeeps limping and holding one arm. "In!" someone shouted and shoved her. She got in. They loaded the shot rock thrower in with her, he was in her lap like a sack and bleeding. The jeep did a U turn and was out of the zone in a screech and some dust. The two men in front radioed ahead so people were waiting at the aid station, including an ambulance for the kid. They took her inside.

A doctor came up, unbuttoned her, pulled her blouse down, saw the gouge the stone made, felt for the bone while she winced, then rolled her on the table, pulled her skirt up and her panties down and looked at the gouge in her buttocks, then he rolled her again to look at her thigh. "All bad bruises," he said to someone. "No worry with antiseptics. Throw some on and get rid of her." He walked away. A corpsman then applied the antiseptics, rolling her around also as so much meat, scarcely noticing her body, which was a fine one apart from the gouges. "Okay," he said. She covered herself and got painfully off the table. Her camera and bag were on a chair. The whole mood of the place was like bracing for a hurricane or a tidal wave. She sat in the chair for a minute, but not on the half of her that hurt. There was no feeling out there, there was hatred, and a cold purpose.

Another jeep roared up and the doctor was back in the dispensary. This was an Arab woman and she'd been hit with something somewhere. She had the chador on and a long gown and as the doctor started to pull the chador off her head she hit him. And he hit her back and pulled the cloth free. Sure enough the back of her head had been opened by a rubber bullet graze. She bit the doctor's hand as he tried to test the wound. So he grabbed her arm, twisted it so she rolled face down on the table, then took a good look at the wound. "We clean, we stitch, she pulls it out, it's her head." So he gave the arm to his aid, went around, held her head firm in one hand and, one handed, cleaned the wound as she jerked in spasms, then stitched the wound as she jerked some more. "Okay," he said, "put some cuffs on her at least until the antiseptic takes. And stick her in a chair where she can't hit her head. You, lady, out of that one. I told you to get lost."

"Get another one," the lady said, "I can do more than bite."

"Okay," he said, "other chair, sit it here, near the lady, one woman to another."

They cuffed the woman to a chair next to the lady. She was twisting and turning her neck as if trying to get rid of anything her enemy had put in it. And she was spitting in hatred. At one point the doctor sprayed her stuck out tongue with something and she went into a fit of sneezing. Then a flood of injured started to come in. The doctor did a quick diagnosis, broken this, hospital, broken that, we fix it here, then take him to jail. All were young men. Except the last, a young girl, maybe ten, her arm limp, broken from a bullet hit. "Up on the table," the doctor said, and two soldiers hoisted her to a sitting position. The doctor looked. "I need an x-ray," he said. So two aids took the girl who kicked one of them.

The woman seated by the lady kicked the other as he backed. And he gave her a kick in return, enough almost to break her shin with the steel toe of the boot. She cringed in pain. Then went back to spitting curses. The doctor sprayed her into sneezes again. Then he went to several patients to check splints and casts. His aids brought the x-rays of the young girl's arm. "Okay, it'll heal," he said, "we knock her out, put a cast on shoulder to wrist. They'll have to bust her arm to get it off."

The woman tried to rise with the chair. The doctor shoved her back down. Then he grabbed her by the jaw so she couldn't bite and took a look at the stitched wound. "Okay," he said, "another hour and it'll stay clean." Then, "You, lady, you see enough yet? You want to follow her home and see them pull the stitches out and spit on the wound? To get rid of what we did? You want to follow this kid home and see them bust the cast? Damn if she goes through life with a useless arm!"

"Why don't you let their doctors do it?" the lady asked.

"They haven't got enough," the doctor said. "They know it. And some wounds you have to act fast on."

"This is all meat to you," the lady said.

"Right," the doctor said. "Has to be. If I treated their souls, you'd hear a different howl."

"You couldn't treat their souls," the lady said.

The doctor looked at her. "You could?" he asked. "Stick to the meat approach. You can respect them some." He looked away. "Okay for the kid?" He spent the next twenty minutes doing a careful cast on the girl's arm. Meantime there was a lot of commotion outside the door. Relatives were showing up, of the woman, of the girl. "Okay," the doctor said, "I want some rifles showing. You, lieutenant, you want to let these people go? Okay, they go. Wrap that woman's head in a bandage. Scare 'em a bit outside so they're afraid to pull it off for a while. Here, sit the girl and let her wake some more. You, lady, you on your own?"

"What are you," she said, "Jekyll and Hyde?"

"No," he said, "I keep things alive. Even my enemies. The meat approach. Live meat, not dead. Dead stinks and everybody leaves it. I get through someday. Someday nobody spits on what I stitch or put in a cast. Someday people will love the meat. You have nice meat. Why break it with a rock in three places? Why break it with a bullet? Why not wag tongues? Tongues are good meat. You ready, lieutenant? Let the girl's people in first. They'll scoop her right out of here." The lieutenant opened the door and things happened exactly as the doctor said, her people grabbed the girl, she screamed with the hurt, but they did not heed, they just swept her through the door. "Okay," the doctor said, "I need a chair." He got one. He held it out as a lion tamer does. "Loose the cuffs." A young soldier did. Another opened the door. Several people rammed in and grabbed the woman not knowing she was trying to get at the doctor and they wrestled her out the door.

"Okay, now you, lady, I haul you someplace," he said, "I have to report and hit a hospital. Day's over here, no more news." He hitched a gun belt around his waist, big 45 in it, then put on a field jacket. She really couldn't get up from two of the bruises. So he reached down and grabbed her arm, swung it around his neck and lifted her. "Walk on the good leg," he said. She just about did, out to the jeep where she looked in fear at the metal seat. He lifted her under the knees and simply deposited her on the seat and she rolled a bit on the unharmed buttock. He got in and drove.

"Where?" he said. She gave her press office address. "Twenty minutes," he said, "that's back in a safe place." She winced at a bounce. He slowed. "You don't fight me anymore," he said. She said nothing. "You fight me in print," he continued. "I read I am an animal. I go off and die of shame. You ride blond stallion with long hair and three bruises showing. The whole world loves your ass."

"I have never met anyone so crude in my whole life," the lady said.

"So, not the woman in the chair?" he said back. "She got her hands on me, you know what she'd cut off?"

"Then why touch her?" exploded the lady.

"Same reason I touch you," he said. "We're all the same meat. Nobody dies if I can help it. I heal. I keep healing. Somebody wakes up. Nobody dead wakes up. We're all beasts here. So I drug the lion before I fix its teeth."

"You mean they are beasts," the woman said.

"No, I mean we are, we all are," the man said as he swung the jeep toward west Jerusalem.

"You could go away," she said.

"Not with what I know," the man said.

"How can you not?" she sputtered out.

He pulled over. "Listen, when your own flesh and blood is killing your own flesh and blood you don't go away." He was quivering. "I don't have to be gentle. And you don't have to be a fake." He drove out again. He said nothing until he got to the press office address, pulled over and stopped. "You climb down okay?" he asked.

"No," she said. So he came around and lifted her out.

"Got it clear now?" he said still holding her up.

"Yes," she said, "you're both beasts."

"Right." he said. "Now what? She said nothing.

"Stitches," he said, "and casts. And take the bullets out." He got back in the jeep and made to drive off.

"You don't shoot!" she shouted at him.

"Were you shot?" he asked, and moved the jeep very slowly, giving her a chance to answer. She had none. So he left.

Trinity Sunday

Feast or Famine

The Spirit and our spirit bear united
witness that we are children of God. And
if we are children we are heirs as well:
heirs of God ...
          —Romans 8:14,17

She was a widow, he was a widower, they had both lost farms, and were at a church bazaar that made money to help people. "So come live with me," he said, "two is cheaper and I can cook."

"They'd think we're shacking up," she said.

"Look at us," the man said, "Guinness book of records if we could. I just miss talk."

"I don't," she said, "but I don't mind it. I like the motion of things. Even the swaying of the house on storm nights. Like muscles on a dancer. You remember that Russian on TV? He looked like knotted ropes. And he had sex on him like a melon. My sons, when they were little, used to say buy him for the cows."

"I remember," the man said. "I liked him. Mine thought he was a soft pear. Looked hard but would squish. So I have this winterized cabin and this jeep. And myself to talk to."

"You have an idea," she said. "Now there's a pumpkin pie made by someone young, cracked right at the navel. So eat around the outside and it'll be great, the middle will be bland. Like to poke it and make it giggle."

"Never liked pumpkin," the man said. "She did and thought I did. I'm a great fake when there's no big issue."

"So you're apple?" she asked.

"Am I!" he said.

95

"Here's apple," she said, and she picked it up. "Light. Oh, someone's good. Lay some cheese beside it." She put it down. "My men all moved quietly. I guess from me. But the sons were meant for school, so that's what they are, both principals. Show them prairie and they shiver. I get to go east twice a year. And come back with bad lungs."

"So when will you move in?" the man asked.

"Need a minute to think," she said. "We give up all this, church and prayers and pies."

"I couldn't marry," he said, "it's not that, it's new, it's like you feel at home with a land, then the land is gone, then you feel at home with someone, and the land is back, though it's not yours."

She started to laugh very quietly and looked at him. "Land," she said, "we can't wash it off can we? We're nothing and its everything." She put a hand on his arm and started moving him towards the preserves table. "We never minded old impotence, did we?" she continued. "I let some cows die. They fed us so much. Husband didn't like it, but I used to hang something on them where there'd be a bell, something of mine so he saw the likeness."

"We're really low," he said, "like a couple of tires." They stopped in front of the preserves. "That's really us. Someone loves berries." He picked up a jar. The homemade wax on top.

"So what would you want to talk so much about?" she asked. "I mean would you drive us both crazy talking about what we lost?"

"No," he said. "I made up my mind to talk about the future."

"We haven't really got one," she said, "so I guess I'd have my silence."

"Well, we do," he said, "we just don't know it."

"I'm not a school person," she said, "but I know nonsense."

"Well," he said, "we could talk about the scandal we caused. And how to handle the phone calls. And excommunication. I think we'd see how funny people think."

"Oh, but there'd be no peace," she said. "And you know how empty you get when you laugh too much. Look at this hard sauce. It just jumps off the spoon."

"You know," he said, "I feel the future is like winter wheat and it's been a dry year and it's better to plough it under."

"We are left no choices," she said. "I know what you mean." She turned him the other way and took his other arm and steered him toward the special breads, raisins, carraway seeds, fruit bits, glazed toppings. "So I've decided to go into the river. Like one last baptism. White gown. Garland around my head. But there'll be no tadpoles. When I was baptized first, it was in spring, in a pond, and I was all tadpoles when I surfaced, they were stuck to me like bees."

"Oh," he said, "you don't look *that* down. I thought you just looked unused."

"I'm *that* down," she said. "Except for you, and just for your moving, not for your talk, though that's nice, it's got a navel to it, no need for a poke."

"I held a barn up once," he said. "This is honey bread. Eat it without tea. A thing I should have fixed, but it was ancient, so I prayed it up, until one day I went in for the tractor and it started to lean. It was going forward. So I backed the tractor against a beam then kept backing until it was upright. It could have gone several ways. Then I went out and roped it to a tree, you wouldn't believe. So I get my tractor out, the rope snaps and down it comes, slowly like a tent. But great old wood. It's what I used for the cabin I live in. So don't."

"It's the best solution," she said. "A little harm at first, then a lot of good. And I'm back with nature as something. I wish I could feed it milk. Bones'll have to do. Potassium." They moved along the breads to the relishes. He had her by the arm now. Then they came to fruit, white pears, pink peaches, apricots in mason jars. "I got your tongue," she said.

"You did," he said, "it's like I'm dropping through space and everything is quiet. Like before snow. Then it starts to drift down and things are even quieter. I used to go out near the corn stalks to hear if there was a sound when the flakes hit, and there wasn't."

"I will go that way," she said, and she turned one of the mason jars to see the peach halves better. "I think they're a little hard."

"Well, I had a future ten minutes ago," he said.

"I think you liked the stalks more than the snow or the silence," she said.

"I did," he said. "Those strange things with their arms out like the old Sioux on horseback praying Manitou or whoever."

"It's a lifeless life," she said.

"But it's there," he said, "and it makes sense. All winter long you can see where the rows were, you can see where you'll go next spring. Even dead they're alive if you look right."

"So I'm not to go into the river?" she said.

"No, you're not," he said.

"I just stand here and mark something for next year? And next year?"

"Yes," he said, "but not too many. Ground blows away if you don't plant new."

"Where will you be?" she asked.

"Where I can see you," he said. "If church, church; if bazaar, bazaar; my house, your house."

"I never thought of being a stalk," she said, "like a Sioux, arms up, to somebody."

"You take people with you," he said.

2nd Sunday, Ordinary Time

Like Somebody's Earrings

You are not your own property; you
have been bought and paid for.
—I Cor. 6:20

"I heard the voice of God once," a young man was saying. "It told me to go away and leave people alone. Before that I thought God was Church. So you mentioned getting married in Church and I said I have to tell you no. And you don't know that side of me."

"I don't," she said, his fiancé, and she looked pale. She had thought he was within her belief. "I am not going outside for a husband," she said. There was a shake in her voice. She loved this man. "God does not say such things as go away."

"So I shouldn't tell you," he said, very quietly, as if to end things. But they were glued to each other, until some question was resolved.

"If I listen to you, you will harm me," she said. "So be silent. And I will love you. And the Church will hold you as I will."

"Alright," he said, and she could feel the love across the table.

"No, not alright," she said in a whisper as if to herself. "You've set something loose in me, it's like a rip, or rocks coming down, you made me love you and now I'm . . ." she couldn't say. "It's what they say the devil does, breaks you in pieces with something good." She was moving her head left and right as if to free her neck from a knot. "It was the devil that told you to go away and leave people alone." He said nothing. "But who's telling *me* to go away and leave *you* alone? Someone is, leave him, someone says, find a mate of your own cloth." She was really quivering now. "I can't leave him, I am saying to someone. I love him or I don't exist."

"I will change to you," he said.

ant

ant

"No, you won't," she said. "Oh, you'll do it so no one will know, but I will, you will not be what I love." The words were surprising her as they came out. "Someone has gotten hold of my voice," she went on, leaning towards him. She took him by the wrists. "It's like I'm possessed by another voice." There was fear on her face now. "Am I being taken over?" He said nothing. "Tell me" she said, "is this a deadly love?"

"You mean could it kill us both?" he asked.

"No," she said, "I mean is it born of the devil?"

"How can I think that?" he asked. "Unless I saw you turn into something evil. And if you're evil, that's all there is." He had turned his hands over on the table so he held her wrists.

"Why did God tell you to go away and leave people alone?" she asked.

"I was doing my missionary years," he answered, "in my nice suit and tie, and I was stopping people on the street and telling them their past was wrong and I could promise them a right future in heaven so they could ignore the oppressions of this world and take suffering as a punishment for sin. And my Spanish wasn't really any good so I don't know what they were hearing, except the sound of pesos I used to peel off this huge roll to buy them bus fare on something. And I was walking down an old boulevard one day and a woman stopped me and asked for bus fare home, 150,000 pesos, about a dime, and I gave it to her, and she looked puzzled. There was no bus stop near. There were some bushes and some barbed wire and a pile of manure, a place behind the bushes where you could make love on the ground, and I hadn't a clue until a hundred yards down the street that I had met someone at work. And that's when the voice came and said go away. I was there for me, my own little shiny beliefs, and I was feeding it stalks like what? a sugar mill? So I've been living for the voice to say stay. I mean I've been trying to let things be. I guess that doesn't work either. And this love has surprised me, and it's taken me over, so you just have to say, and I'll be. But that's not right."

"I won't say," she said, "not anymore." Then she went on, "We're like somebody's earrings."

"I was at home down there only one time," he said, "when I was learning. I had an Aymara Indian as a teacher. And our text book was bad, all about rich kids from Ecuador off shopping for mini-skirts in Miami. I asked him to teach me some other way. So he told me pagan things. And I was shocked for a while, as if he was mocking me. But he wasn't. He talked about the shadows in the valley being the souls of his ancestors, and how his native language had no abstract words, but had words for every possible thing. And I was fascinated and learned the little I did learn that way. He had a beautiful voice and copper skin. And for a while I forgot my message."

"I want to be with you," she said, her voice now very calm. "And I want forgiveness before I am."

"Oh," he said, "you sound like a despair."

"No," she said, "no, it's more hope, it's that I can't mistrust you, the labels don't stick, I haven't anything else I can do, or want to do."

"I can take the blame," he said.

"That'd be a lie," she said. "And I don't want to be blessed and you damned. And that's what I meant when I asked you is this love deadly and are you just moved around?"

"So I haven't really changed," he said. "I'm not my own." He was talking inward towards himself.

"But you do love me?" she asked. There was a long, long time of silence. She slid her hands free of his. "You're stripped of everything now, aren't you?" she said.

"Yes," he said.

"If I leave you, what will happen?" she said.

He waited again a long, long time. "I will be free," he said. His cheeks began to flush. And he began to laugh a little. "Exactly the way you are in this last five minutes." He opened his hands face up on the table. "I was on a micro bus one day," he went on, "it was jammed, it was low, I was in the aisle and forced to bend way down over one of the seats. An Indian woman was suckling her baby and both breasts were bared and it looked as if I was trying to take a drink out of the free one. And I was so embarrassed and glad to get off that bus! But it's the opposite now. It's like a sacred memory. Do you know what I mean?"

"Both of mine are free," she said.

Brains Not Brawn

*Brothers: our time is growing short
...I say this because the world
as we know it is passing away.*
—1 Corinthians 7:29, 31

A woman was thirsty. She'd like a beer. A long day of teaching problem youth for the Town Council. She was a specialist in the violent, and a pub and a pint were treatment for herself. So she went into one in the town, just down the road from the school, put her briefcase against the bar rail and signalled the publican. "A stout, please." He was unnerved a bit, so were the few drinking their own. They knew the world was changed, they couldn't help reverse it. But he drew her a pint and put it on the bar before her and said, "Luck." "Thanks," she said.

"You're the teacher," he said. "Yes," she said. "For the tough ones," he said. "Yes," she said. "How do you ever?" he said. The others had been listening and curiosity got them. They moved a bit down the bar in the woman's direction. "You live it first," she said, "then you think about it. You write a book. And someone says for so many pounds a week will you pet our sharks." She sipped from her pint, the foam made a moustache, she wiped it off with the back of her hand. And they grinned a bit, all of them.

One said, "They say you're a black belt and could break someone with a blow. And they're in fear of a killer woman." "Who says?" another man said, "you're making it up to see something. This bar cracked in two and us dry for a week." "I'm not," the first said, "it was among the women I heard it, I had a bus of them to the shrine for the Holy Mother's feast. And they were saying she could kill, so the boys were tame." "Ah," said the first voice, "they're cracked. Look at this thing, she can hardly lift that pint."

The woman with the pint smiled. "It gets lighter," she said as she took another sip. "And people get lighter the more they talk." A third voice cut in, "You see it?" he said. "It's in the brain not the brawn, she *talks* them slack." "Right," said the woman with another sip. "They're deaf and dumb," the first voice said, "and I'd be, if I had my feet and could run from the Royal beasts." "A bomb tosser," said the second voice, "you'd do it the old way. Olympic games throwing the hammer for TV and a hundred thousand in the stands." "Well, they'd go then," said the first. "You're in a dream," said the second, "so don't you wake up." "You must have a wisdom," said the third. He was empty and nodded to the publican for a fill.

She answered, "Just that a pint in a pub late in the day puts things back in their cages so I don't have to mind. Or sharks back in the pool as I said before." "You're bothering the woman," said the publican putting the refill on the bar, "like horse flies. You'll have her twitching." "You're not bothering me," the woman said. "If they were all like you it'd be daisies and love me, love me not." "God, you're neat," said the third voice. "I had a whippet once that could go through a hedge without a hair lost, the rabbits died of fright." "You don't want bloody details," the woman said now two thirds through her stout, "you wouldn't enjoy another drop." "Well, you're a puzzle," said the first voice, "and what else have we to do?"

She was leaning one elbow on the bar now, and her body showed in its form under the loose clothes and they were reminded of themselves and grew self conscious. "Is that it?" said the third voice. "You get them on to a different pleasure? They say Hannibal, you know, could get the boy elephants on the raft to cross the river by putting the girl elephants on first." "Only in part," said the woman. "They're as frightened of pleasure as you are." They were silent.

"And you've no need to be frightened," the woman went on, now near the bottom of her glass. "You show them that you do not fall for their violence. You keep asking them to explain it to you as you stand there in your woman's body and they see they make no sense. Then they move to wipe you out. And that's when they discover their choice. If they ruin me, they go mad. Have you ever seen anyone who chose to go mad? I don't mean drift into it. I mean choose it? Knowing they will never come back out?"

"How do you know such things?" the third voice said with his new pint untouched.

"From just standing here and drinking a stout," she said. "But more than that," she went on. "I have brothers. They were going out one night to hit something. And they killed the innocent in a church hall and were sorry, blaming it on the fuse that was defective and went off too early. Oh, no one knew their names or that they phoned the newspapers with the excuse. And I'm telling you something that puts you in danger if you open your mouths. They were cool afterwards, in and out of the house, as if they were doing their sums. So I came to the three at table and said kill me now because I am going to tell who did that bombing. I came from my room in a light robe so they could see their sister's body inside it. And my parents, old rebels the two, were dumbstruck. When you kill your own woman-flesh you have to know you will go crazy after. So the oldest said, 'If I have to, I will!' You have to, I said, and I dropped that robe to the ground. And they were enraged to the point of madness when the youngest, the one closest in age to me, saw. He's strong. Stronger than the others, big, big young man, and he shouted to them to sit. And he said to me, 'You must give us a choice, some other than this.' Because he saw the rest of his life as crazed. And I said if you go away all three, and stay away all three, and never kill more, I will be silent. Well he took my robe. But he kissed my shoulder before he put it on me again. I was everybody's body in that instant. And that's how I learned. And that's the book I wrote, though it's all theory and there isn't a name given away. But you know names now. And you have power. And see how close you are to the same brink if you tell."

She moved her empty glass toward the publican and opened her shoulder purse to pay. "You're money's no good," said the publican. "Please," she said. "No," he said, "my privilege." "Thanks," she said, and turned and left. "A killer," said the first voice, "the women don't know the half."

Outside Disneyland

But the prophet who presumes to say in
my name a thing I have not commanded
him to say, or who speaks in the name of
other gods, that prophet shall die.
—Deuteronomy 18:20

"I've been voodooed," a woman said to a priest over the phone. "Father Solomon, I've been voodooed and someone told me to call you and you would know." His name was not Solomon, but never mind. "How did you find out?" he asked. "Woman told me she saw and I feel my skin coming off me, it's ready to fall like my clothes and there is lye ready for my flesh so I will be only a skeleton and chased away."

"You near a church?" the priest asked. "Yes," she said. "I mean a catholic church?" the priest went on, "one with a crucifix of the dying Jesus?" "Yes," she said. "Well, you go in the front door." "Yes," she said. "And you hold your arms out from your side." "Yes," she said. "And you walk two steps forward and one step back." "Yes," she said. "So the voodoo has to do the same." "Yes." "But he gets left in front every time one step." "Yes." "Until you reach the front." "Yes." "And you know the opening in the altar rail?" "I know." "You take one step inside." "Yes." "Arms still out." "Yes." "Then you go to take another." "Yes." "But you don't, you make believe." "Yes." "You step back instead." "Yes." "The voodoo gets stuck. Gets stuck inside the altar rail." "I don't know." "I do, I do, gets stuck inside with Jesus." "Yes." "Can't get out, has to voodoo Jesus, has to stick to Jesus." "Yes." "You back down the aisle, your arms are down, you're not there." "Yes." "You do that?" "Yes," she said. "Call me after?" the priest said. "Yes," the woman said and the phone went down.

"You fooled with someone," a student said. She was sitting across from the priest in his office. She was writing a paper for his course. He was a teacher too. "Yes," he said. The student looked very hurt. "Voodoo," the priest said. "You still fooled," she said, and very timidly. He looked out the window away from her and over the palm trees towards the river. He could see the superstructure of a ship moving through above the tops a mile a way. Then he looked back at her and broke into a big smile, "Neat, though, huh?"

"What if it doesn't work?" the student said. "I think up something else," the priest said. "I keep her busy so the voodoo doesn't work." "You could damn yourself this way," the student said. "Listen," the priest said, "if there's voodoo, there's a devil, if there's a devil, I have no power, it's God and devil and no one as big as either. So I send her to God." The student looked very puzzled. "I just set it up," the priest continued, "so she'd be near God, never mind the scenario. And if there's no devil, this is all in peoples' heads." "Isn't that too smart?" the student asked. "Sort of like not having to pay if anything goes wrong?"

"Why are you asking me these things?" the priest said, but said very gently. "Because I've been prayed over," the student said, "and I know what went out of me, and you should have prayed over her, not made her do something foolish." The student was flushed with feeling. "There wasn't something in her," the priest said, "voodoo's from outside." The student would not stop. "They make you do things, flesh things, they own you and they run you." She paused. "Then someone puts two hands on you and says the Spirit and it's like people inside you rushing for the door. Then there is fresh air and it's like you dance to yourself, but you know someone dances with you. And you do not do flesh things anymore." "I'm glad for you," the priest said. "You're like a chameleon," she said, "I used to hold one in my hand to see it change and change."

"You might not hear a word I said," the priest replied. "I don't give a hoot for devils. But I give a hoot for people. And I don't like zapping either way. And as I say this to you, I may make you doubt what happened to you. And you may lose the dance and the one who dances with you. Then if there's a devil, it's me." "Yes," she said. She was now staring at him. "But if there's a dance in the self already, and God was always danc- ing with it, but we had wrapped ourselves in chains marked made somewhere else and someone comes along and says, 'My, what marvelous chains, I didn't know you could make chains! What are you up to?' And you say, 'They're made somewhere else.' And someone says, 'But there is no lock!' And you look, you get up to look, and the chains fall!"

"Am I that much of a simp?" the student said, "as much as the one who talked to you on the phone?" "Yes," the priest said. "Then you are a devil," she said. "But I'm one you can handle," he said, "your mind is working now." "How?" she asked. "Matching columns. Me on oneside. Devil on the other. Do we really match?" The student said nothing. "Well?" the priest asked. "Not so you'd notice," the student said. "Thanks," said the priest, and a grin was back on his face.

The phone rang. It was the voodooed woman. "Your skin still on?" the priest asked. "Okay, good, and what about that lye waiting to make you a skeleton? . . . Waiting where? . . . Then you're not going near that market, are you? . . . Well, Jesus can take it if He's got it, can't kill him anymore. He just looks bad. Fools them now. They can't look inside where He's all glory. Yes, yes, you call me. They'll be mad and use more pins but there are holes in Jesus, He sucks those pins in like a rug cleaner, yes, nobody but God, nobody owns, only God. . . Right, so call. Bye."

The student was pale when he hung up. "You think it's Disney World," she said. "Yes, I do," the priest said. "But that woman isn't, her skin and bones are not, her voice on the phone, not Disney World at all." "Ahhh," the student said expelling her breath and shaking her head to get rid of a knock on it, "you just manipulate!" "The opposite," he said. "I've let my guard down with you. I go with people. But when I see a mind show, what I am can come into play. And then there's God. But outside Disneyland. You almost die."

To Be Near a Woman

I made myself all things to all men
in order to save some at any cost.
—1 Corinthians 9:22

A woman had a ham cooking and her thesis open on the kitchen table and her dog scratching at the door to get in. The phone rang. Her husband. Car broke down near the toll gate. He'd get a tow but be home late. Have the two kids get a cab back from skating. "Whew," he said, "you're the only one out of danger." "Maybe not," she said, "my thesis director doesn't like this chapter on Sappho. He says change it or get lost." "I'll have him towed too," the man said. There were clinks from the coins in the pay phone. "Time's up," he said quickly, "here goes." She was cut off saying "Stay with the car, I'll . . . need it later," she finished to herself.

"Sappho, lovely Sappho," she said, "you want to be a man so you can have the woman." The dog scratched again and whined a bit. He knew she was there. She got up and let him in. He headed for the water and lapped for a furious ten seconds, then looked around for applause. She was back with Sappho. "Oops, school," she thought, dialed it on the phone, had the secretary get on the loudspeaker to the outdoor skating rink telling the two girls to cab it home.

There was a loud bang down the street, must be a truck, the lights went out and the stove off. "Ahh," she said, and headed for the front door. Damn if it wasn't a light company truck that had skidded on a patch of ice and taken out a pole. She closed the door, house would be cold. "It's really poetry," she thought, "she's beyond lesbian here. This stuff is delicious, she was so free, the words so formed, not stuck like a bee in its own honey. I thought he saw this!" The lights flicked on. Then flicked out again. Phone rang. The two girls. They'd go with a friend's mother, have supper,

108

practice some cheerleading, then come home. "Okay," she said knowing the ham mightn't cook.

The phone rang again as she put it down. Husband. "Someone ran into the tow," he said fuming, "car looks like a coke can crushed." "You weren't in it?" she blurted. "No," he said, "I was up in the truck. But we had to pull a kid out and I cut my hands on the glass. So I'm going with the cops over to the hospital. I'll see your mother for you." "You'll scare her," the woman said. "I'll keep my hands in my pockets," he said. "Like King Kong," she said, "you're sure you're okay?" Clunk went the coins, the operator saying cut off, him saying phone you. She hung up and the lights went on, so did the stove, and the chapter on Sappho on the table looked like someone hungry who didn't dare ask the time of dinner.

"So you stroked the poem," the woman said as she sat again to the text. "And everyone else has since." She got a little more modest, "Well, everyone who could read Greek." She could. Her father had taught her. With pain. She was bright, bright, but not a boy, and she did best on the passages in Homer about grass and trees and the lovely vales of Thessaly, also the seduction scene in heaven that made Olympus blossom. She was wretched with slaughter scenes, where the spears went in, which eye, which mouth, what splattered on the ground afterwards. When he had skipped her through the lyric poets to get to the tragedies, she had halted and tasted the beauty of Sappho, and that frightened him so he began to throw boys her way.

Her own husband came not thrown. He sat beside her on a bus and she was reading the Loeb *Greek Lyric Poets*. He spotted it and said, "I want you for your body," and grinned hugely. She was anything but body, she played the Wicked Witch of the West in several school performances. "It's not as bad as you think," she had muttered. "I want you for your mind," he then said. That made her look up. And there was this guy that looked like a girl, blond hair, blue eyes, beautiful dimples, and white, white teeth. And he had a soft voice. And was very tall, and very well built. She just started to laugh. "You have to take both," she had said. His mouth made a round O, she thought she'd die seeing it, it was so kissable. "Mind's really too much," he said, "I can scarcely read English, never mind Greek." He had reached a fine soft hand to open the book a bit, she had closed it on her fingers. She knew he was smart. She flushed a little with anger. Which he sensed. So he said, "I need someone real," and he took his hand back. It was like a statement from the brink.

So they began to do a lot together. Her father was now doubly scared about offspring, two-way offspring. But her husband was a glorious form inside and out, he sold clothing to men and women, and forgot to cash his checks. She was glad Sappho wasn't around to meet him. But he was the source of her insight, you can just love a form and it's all itself and not some big deal about nature.

Phone rang. "I scared your mother," he said. "So I told her I was a hero wading through broken glass to save a helpless driver instead of a helpless drunk. That guy was gurgling with alcohol when we hauled him out. Lucky nobody lit a match or his breath would have been a flame thrower. I'm on my way in the cop car so distract the neighbors. Set off some fireworks in the back yard." "Lady Godiva," she said. "Oh no!" he said, "that's for my eyes only." Then he drew in his breath, she could hear it over the phone, "Except if you need a doctor, okay?" "Okay," she said. He hung up.

Something was burning. "Ham," she said and jumped across to the oven door, pulled it open, pulled out the tray, then turned off the electricity. So now ham and raisin sauce and yams and spinach. And Sappho. "All anything needs is a quick heat," she thought, "but they won't be hungry." She pulled a strip off the top of the ham and sat back at the table to the poem. "She wanted to be a man to be near that woman," she said aloud to her absent thesis director. "She would take on any form to love any form. She was up in the realm of love. A dog to love a dog. A devil to love a devil. Don't you understand, you poor, frightened man? Okay, I'll grant you a footnote, the poem is a substitute for sex and that diminishes its lyric liberty, so some say." She wrote it on a pad of paper, she could enter it in the computer later. "But it's a love of its own, this poem, it's exquisite."

A string of ham was stuck to her teeth, it made her want more. She turned to the ham in time to see the dog nibbling at a corner of it. Who then slunk back under her menacing gaze. Her tibetan lamasery dog who never barked, just the soft whine and only for her when she didn't answer his scratch at the door. Long gray hair. The phone rang. The girls. To stay overnight and come by before school in the morning for a change. "Okay, but be sure," she said. Phone rang again. "Listen," he said, "Police want me to identify this kid before a judge. He's a lot more than a drunk driver. Two hours maybe, I'll grab a Big Mac." "With what" she asked, "your two paws?" "I have the massive jaws of a primate," he said, "fearsome. Bye."

She was alone then with Sappho for the evening. "So I'll betray you in a footnote. So he won't see what you really are. And he won't put *his* paws on you." She thought of her husband and his bandaged hands. "Anytime," she thought. And she saw his round mouth forming an O, and the dimples, and the blue eyes, the brows and blond hair. And she heard the soft sounds of licking. Her silent dog at the ham.

The Death of Stinky

*A man infected with leprosy must wear
his clothing torn and his hair disorder-
ed; he must shield his upper lip and
cry, "Unclean, unclean."*
—Leviticus 13:45

"They used to tack a quarantine to the door in those days," a man was saying. The drink was shaking in his hand. He lived around that shake very well. A kidney shaped pool in front of him, a house like a broken C around the pool, one floor, deep and cool, palm groves at either end and azaleas crowded to the edge of each sliding door. Some friends were over, an old stock broker buddy and his new wife whose money was from a jewelry first husband she had buried a year ago. The talk was about typhoid down in the one poor section of the desert where the service people lived.

"Geez it was scary to me as a kid, like the inside of the house was filled with germs, one inch in that door and you'd get it, scarlet fever, whooping cough, consumption, God! I haven't thought of that word in years. Everybody died of consumption because we couldn't say the big word and have it mean something. So I used to scuff along faster to school and the nun would skip the name of one empty chair and we knew. You ever see an empty chair and desk in one of those old parochial schools?"

"I went to synagogue," the old stock broker buddy said. "We had these long benches and they'd cram us in. Kids would squirt off either end but you'd never know in the middle. There was this one stinky kid, I'll never forget it, we tumbled around like monkeys to get away from him, or we'd squeeze left or right and kids would tumble off the end until we had him at the end so only one of us suffered. God, I haven't thought of that in years either."

"We must all have been crawling with germs," the first man said, "tough little buggers." And he took a sip of satisfaction from his drink which rattled in his hand so he giggled. "I can still thread a needle," he said wiping some scotch off his chin. "But I have to trick myself. I give the command right and I move left, funniest damn thing."

"You know," the old buddy said, "that Stinky, he wrote stuff for Hollywood and McCarthy got him for being a commie and he killed himself, but sent a letter before he did to come find him, and he was dead on top of every book in the house torn apart, it was like a dump, and he took rat poison." "What was that all about?" the shaky guy said. "I don't know," said the old buddy, "why waste all that energy ripping stuff up if you're gonna go, and sleeping pills, go out sweet, but Stinky had to go out stinky I guess."

"You dumb men," the woman said. "He was calling everything trash. You too. Me too." She said little, this woman. She played great bridge and poker and was a genius cook and could listen to drones talk by the hour and not listen so her soul was placid. "No," her husband said, "he was always stinky, he couldn't think of anything else."

"Maybe *she's* right," the shaky guy said, "but *he* ain't right. We beat all those diseases so why crap on us? Remember polio? The Russians beat that? We did, a dime at a time. Cripes a dime was a movie and it hurt but we gave it. March of dimes. Remember those iron lungs and you'd see the guy in the mirror just over his head? Then the shots, gone polio, then the sulfa, gone, what? gonorrhea, oh baby! people don't know, we had all kinds of words for that and people used to go crazy when they got older. One wild night when they were twenty and no brains left when they were sixty. There was like a fear and we used to whisper in the eighth grade that the girl in the third row had it. But girls never suffered we thought, just the guy she gave it to. Gone, penicillin and gone! And what else did the commies didn't do? So Stinky stank a lot more than he thought."

"We did nothing," the woman said, "was scientists did it. Some were kids of Russian Jews. One Armenian I think. Never know in this country." "Wait," her old buddy husband said, "then why didn't they do it back there?" "Yeah," the shaky man said, "because there's fresh air here, I mean you can use your mind, American air like, back there everybody was in Siberia except Uncle Joe and a few stooges. Until the war when they had to use people to stop bullets." "Be nice men," she said, "and use *your* brains in this nice air. Human beings they were sometimes. Human beings we were not sometimes." "What's with the human being?" the shaky man asked. He really didn't follow her. The old buddy husband broke in, "She's Jewish from Lithuania. She had to choose between the Russians and the Germans. So she ran west. Some Russians helped her. Some Germans. Some Americans didn't. So she looks for human beings, forget it where they're from." "So human beings make the medicines," the shaky guy said, "is that what?"

"Nice mind," she said, "nice man. But listen. You have to worry again. Penicillin does not work so well any more. Sex germs are smart too." The shaky man started to laugh. "My wife's up in heaven looking at me," he said. "Good woman. Jealous woman. She used to phone me when I was on the road so if I was in bed with somebody that'd spoil it. I mean like two in the morning. But I was never interested in that stuff. So I'd answer and geez didn't she have to pretend there was something important. I think she was the world's best liar on the spot. I used to write them down so I'd catch a repeat and she never repeated. I built this place without walls inside except for the jakes so she could see me every minute. So she sees every minute now, I bet, let God go play golf by himself."

"What if *all* the germs are smart?" the old buddy said. "We'll be back to nailing quarantines on the door, stay away or die, all you who pass by. Rhymes! Where'd I hear that?" "Gone dumb again," said the woman. "We're too old to catch. Those things for kids." "Yeah?" the old buddy said, "well we got some things kids ain't got." He finished his drink and put a grin on for another. The shaky guy said, "Yeah, yeah, I forgot, listen, there's plenty and it's lonely. You too?" he said to the woman. "I can't pour even so you do it. I have to splash. Cat gets up there sometimes."

And he rose with them to refill his drink. "You ever see a cat drunk?" "This is the best medicine ever invented," the old buddy said as he poured the purest scotch into an empty glass. "Now," he said, "the smallest ice cube and you watch it tickle. Like that fusion fission we saw on TV." "Wrecks your liver," the woman said as she poured too. "But why not? Liver is not brains."

7th Sunday, Ordinary Time

Cops and Crooks

*I it is, I it is, who must blot out
everything and not remember your sins.*
—Isaiah 43:25

He heard them fighting. All the time now. They forgot his birthday. Eight years old. She was saying not to touch somebody or she'd leave. He was saying she had flipped. Watched too much TV. There was something good on now. It was about otters and how they played with everything. There was a skunk and two otters and they just wanted to tickle the skunk but he let go and the two otters were rubbing themselves on everything. But she screamed she wasn't dumb and get out right now and he shouted not for a crazy woman. There was a kid to care for she'd ruined already and what if he heard. So their voices lowered to strangled words from his mother and curses to himself from his father and things slammed but under great control. So he turned to the next channel where he knew the Jungle Book was on and this one had a bear, some bees, honey and some squirrels watching the bees attack the bear.

He heard the sound of a fist landing and his heart nearly stopped. There were no words out there, there was no movement. The bear and bees were gone and there was a Cheerios ad on with peaches being sliced into the bowl, then a long column of delicious milk falling into it without splashing. And still no sound from outside the door. He went on all fours and listened. He was going to get it for this. He was really the bad one. He had left his breakfast and that started the fight because he was undisciplined. And she said, "You're never home enough to see, you're out ploughing someone else's turf." "I'm paying for your life of liesure," he had said, "and you can't take care of one kid." "Bring your others home," she had said. The boy wanted brothers and sisters. He was talking to himself all the time at

116

home, and it didn't work at school where he got kicked a lot instead of the ball and the girls screeched and ran from him. It was so quiet outside the door. He had gotten hit but it was like flapping water with a flipper. He raised up on his knees and turned the knob so they wouldn't notice and pulled the door slowly toward him. There was no air to breathe. He saw his mother holding her hand to her face and his father standing with his mouth open and his hands down and they were not breathing either, so he closed the door and looked for someplace to go. The TV was on to some birds chasing a crow through the trees and the bed was all rumpled and there was no room in the closet.

But the window was open out onto the porch and his two wheeler was left out from yesterday. So he went through the window without opening it any more and making noise and went over the porch railing and down onto the soft loam of the flower bed. He knew he was crying but he could still ride, the sidewalks until he got to the park, then he could go for a long time without cars until he reached the river where he would have to stop. But he heard a shot fired from back inside the house and he froze in panic at the rear of the driveway away from the street. He was transfixed by the silence inside. And it went on and on. Until he heard the sound of a siren off in the distance, a siren that got closer and closer and whoopier and whoopier as he stood there holding his bicycle unable to move. There were several sirens now and they all joined at the end of the street and came up it, screeching to a halt in front of the house. Ambulance and cruisers, people rushing toward the door he couldn't see, his mother's voice saying, "Please, I'm sorry," drifting around the corner. The radios were crackling furiously, more cruisers arrived, and he just stood there with bicycle completely forgotten.

There was another burst of activity as the ambulance pulled out into the street, then backed right up over the sidewalk nearly to the front steps. They were loading his father onto it, and the police were bringing his mother who had tried to stop his father's bleeding. The ambulance had the two of them and she looked out the window as it pulled away and saw him with his bicycle toward the rear of the house and she turned for help but the ambulance swept out of view down the street. He let the bicycle fall away from him but didn't move, there was nowhere to go. The cruiser's radio crackled again, then a policeman rounded the house looking for him, big heavy gun in his holster on one side, big walkie talkie hooked on the other, and cuffs hanging down in front then the claw in its special clasp. So he ran, ran behind the next house, then out to the sidewalk toward the park and the river, but the cruiser passed him and pulled up and the policeman jumped out and put his hands up in the air like somebody surrendering.

The boy stopped running because he couldn't breathe and cry. He sat on the sidewalk. He saw the policeman take off the gun and throw it away with its holster, over some bushes into some bigger bushes. Then he threw his walkie talkie after it. Then other things too. He walked toward the boy with his hands out wide and empty. Then he reached down and lifted him to his feet but he couldn't stand so he sat down with him on the sidewalk and waited until the sobs began to come then he put an arm around him and rocked with him until all the sobs were gone. Another cruiser slid up smoothly near him and seemed just to wait. There were some crackles from it that were quickly switched off. But the other car radio made menacing noises and the policeman stiffened. He pulled him to his feet and said, "Go with her," and he opened the nearest cruiser's front door. "Go, you'll be cared for." The boy sat and saw the policeman leap the bushes down the street, find his gun, strap it on, then leap back out onto the sidewalk into the other cruiser, flip on the siren and lights and screech a U turn and roar down the street.

The policewoman with the boy was looking at him. He was staring straight ahead like someone afraid to look at her, afraid to look at the world. "You want to drive with me?" she asked. He didn't know what she meant. "You sit here on my lap and drive with me," she said. "We go and stop bad things. We go help people who are hurt." He didn't move. "Come," she said, "you sit here on my lap and you and I drive." She reached a hand and drew him, and he sat in on her lap against her. She put her hands on the wheel and said, "Now put yours on top of mine and follow me and we drive and help people." And he did, he could feel how soft her hands were, how soft a seat she was.

She eased the car away from the curb and did a reverse with his hands following hers. Then she drove slowly past his house, he drove slowly. "We leave it until later," she said. "We fix them up, then we come back. Okay?" He nodded. "We turn here and we go find them. Okay?" They turned out onto the main street. "We fix them up then we drive them back.

Okay?" He nodded. "We find them in the hospital. Okay?" He was watching the road and moving with her hands. "And we tell them not to be bad again. Okay?" He nodded. "You're a good driver," she said, "you want to stay with me?" He shook his head. "You want to stay with them?" He nodded. "Then they'll have to be good. Or we can't bring them home. Okay?" He nodded. "Don't hold the wheel too tight," she said. "Fine. Now turn. Say, I'll take you anytime." He nodded.

8th Sunday, Ordinary Time

Fool, Fool Love!

*I am going to lure her and lead her out
into the wilderness and speak to her
heart.*
—Hosea 2:14

"This funeral is a farce," a woman thought. "We're burying a mean bastard with lilies and lights-out prayers." She looked down the pews towards the front. Her friend, her high school friend, the widow, stood there, her kids to her right, the boys in their late teens, the girl in her middle ones, and she could see the scars on them the liar in the coffin put there. The incredible liar who got his wife on one, his house on several, his law firm on hundreds, his reputation on thousands. He lied to the wrong people finally and here he was riddled with bullets. A fabled figure henceforth. A mafia lawyer who milked their cow on the sly just as he milked the law—fees, fees for every breath he drew. "Meter's busted," she thought. She saw some reporters in the congregation. Rich stuff if they could spot a revealing face. People had to play it normal. As telltale to skip as to come.

She had said no to this man. Many years ago when she was a beauty queen, against her will really, small college and the votes of friends. She sensed the lie, it was a feeling not a judgment, somehow he really didn't want to touch her. Those days the guys went for inside blouses or for thighs under ballerina skirts. She knew he wanted a doll. She had broken a wrist on another guy who thought she was a dog. So twenty years in the convent as a teaching nun just to get free to be herself and not someone's poodle or cabbage patch. But the love there was like a clothesline still in its knots. Meantime her best friend fell for the lie of this dead man and became the doll. So now this funeral and what to do with the debris. She had come out of the convent a year ago and he learned of it. He offerred to help her make up for lost time in bed. Cold still, like someone picking up tourist stickers. So here we are burying him," she thought. "This is where love stops. Whatever there was of it."

There was a sudden sobbing that broke in on the priest's voice as he started the final prayers over the coffin. It did not come from the widow. It came from a woman on the other side of the aisle and it was uncontrollable. She kept saying, "No! No!" in a thick accent, and she sank back onto the pew. There was no one with her. And she was in black with a hat and veil. She was devastated by grief. And she began to keen. People tried to shush her, they looked for someone she might be with. It was a foreign kind of keening too, Mediterranean, and it sent shivers through the mourners and guests. Then something happened. The widow left her pew, crossed the aisle behind the casket and stepped along the kneeler past people until she came to the woman and she reached down and put her arms around the sobbing, keening figure and tried to make her stand but she couldn't. So the widow sat and held the woman who now yielded but let her head turn up toward the ceiling so her throat was clear, her grief deeper in its sound, its hoarse No! No! Then she stood up out of the widow's arms, swept her hat and veil off and let them drop. She ripped open her blouse, her head still towards heaven, pulled the blouse down so her breasts were cleared and trembling and she began to hit herself as if to move God to bring the corpse back to life. And the widow closed behind her, put her arms around her again, so when the grief sound subsided and exhaustion set in the woman collapsed back in her arms and the two sank to the pew. The widow then drew the blouse back up, found the hat, put it on her and draped the veil in front. She looked up towards the priest and said, "Go on." And the priest did, but no one heard his words. The grief of the woman still jammed their nerves.

The woman down in the back was shattered. This is not where love stopped. Someone still loved that bastard! But now the grief of the stricken woman had revived and she struggled out of the bench over people's feet losing her headgear and threw herself on top of the coffin. No wail this time. Just panting like the panting of love, a sucking in and expelling of breath. The widow came up behind her again, reached for her shoulders and drew her upright and held her so the other woman's head was on her shoulder. "Finish," she said to the priest. Then the grief stricken woman began to kiss the widow's hand, just lifted it and began to kiss it, in the palm, then she kissed the other and began to say words to the widow softly, Greek, something, and they seemed like thanks, like kinship words.

The woman down the back saw in a flicker what the scenario was, the last mistress, who could scarcely speak English, who would reveal no secrets, who was brought here as a payoff, a slave in fact, who fell in love with the master, Oh Jesus! because she couldn't know, an arranged marriage, a fake, put up in some flat, thinking he was business on the road, there's maybe a baby, those breasts were loaded. "Oh my God! And maybe my friend knew, the widow maybe knew! Fool, fool love; fool, fool women; fool, fool priest! Fool, fool, God!" And she sat hard on the pew in anger while everyone else stayed standing. She had her fists in her mouth to keep from saying what she thought. "You can only love if you don't know!" Then the cold, sober recognition hit her. "She does know, the cabbage patch doll knows, she knew what that woman was, she knew that woman loved him, Oh God! And now that woman knows something, she's in somebody's arms!" The woman down back stood up again.

The prayers were over and the pall bearers had come to lead the casket down the aisle. But the two women did instead. The widow had turned the mistress and simply taken her by the arm and walked toward the door out to the hearse. The coffin followed. The widow saw her friend down back and saw her anger. Some tears came and she shook her head slightly. No anger. The woman down back nodded, yes, no anger. It all happened so no one else noticed. Then the coffin went by. She blessed herself in the girls' school way, quick, short, like elliptical speech. And she stayed after people filed out, standing. There was bustle up front to strip the altar and put things away. She blessed herself again, this time more slowly. "Don't be fooled," she said. "By me either." And she left.

9th Sunday, Ordinary Time

Where We Go Is a Woman

*We are only earthenware jars that hold this
treasure, to make it clear that such an over-
whelming power comes from God and not from
us.*
—2 Corinthians 4:74

A man was in synagogue on Saturday morning. He came Friday evening too. What he loved was the liesure of it. There was maybe a God out there somewhere working for everybody, he knew that, but here a liesure he could taste. During the rest of the week, look out! His brokerage firm was a noisy place and busy as the Corn Exchange in Chicago. But this crazy liesure tickled his funny bone, like some ultimate defiance of gravity at the top of a dive into a damp rag. And there was a woman rabbi, an assistant, and she was smart, and good looking, but not as good looking as his wife who was upstairs licking stamps for a hospital drive. A wing for the poor in rich-town, maybe just a gesture, but it'd deal with hard cases and pull off some miracles, so why not? Poor buggers could walk back into the ghetto and get hit with another truck or bad needle.

"I'm from a ghetto," he thought, "one old as Methusaleh. I shouldn't vaunt. And brokering's a ghetto, they don't even know their blood types anymore. 'Don't cut your finger ripping off sheets,' I tell 'em, 'we wouldn't know what to pump into you except scotch.' Oh, she's nice!" The woman rabbi was up front showing some visitors around. They had the raw look of the old country. "Old?" he thought. "Younger than I am. Not much." She handed them on to the president who had just come in. Must be important.

She started down the aisle and he waved her to come sit. There were other groups around in pockets. He was back center. It was the best view

123

of the nice wood of the place and the bench to his left where his wife liked
to sit. She tickled him too. She couldn't listen to two words without spinning and whispering. But she was always whispering hot stuff. Not gossip,
she hated that, but buys, houses as well as blouses, and art, did she know
art! especially silk screen stuff which could be beautiful and you didn't
have to insure it too much. She could get commissions but she scorned
them. "One money grubber is enough," she said. "Me. I'm no grubber," he
thought, "Look! I'm doing nothing!" The woman rabbi came down the
bench expecting she didn't know what. She had marvelous breasts with a
life of their own as she did anything involving gesture. He swore they
chased one another like kids under a blanket, himself and his brother when
their mother wanted them up and out to school. Which they both hated because they were ahead of the teacher and had to twiddle most of the day.
He wasn't a sexy guy, he just loved shapes and motions. Nuts about ballet
but he went alone and dressed in Levi's so his colleagues wouldn't see the
glow on his face. They in their suits had to look forebearing.

   "So why this?" he said to her as he asked her to sit with him a minute. "I
love it," she said. His face lit up. "I love it too," he said, "but do I think
something else than you?" She cocked her head as if to say, "Go on." "It's
crazy," he said, "my office is working, my money is working, my wife's
upstairs working, my kids are sailing, and I'm sitting here for nothing, and
it's the nothing I love." "It's not holy to you?" the rabbi asked. "No," he
said, "well, maybe a little, but I don't know holy, except maybe a good
laugh at something really funny, though that can be mean, if something's
stupid and I'm laughing at it." "So Sabbath is funny?" she asked again, the
head cocked in question. "Oh, oh," he said, "I'm sinking. Reach me a
hand."

   She gathered some important sentences in her head, and he drew up in a
pupil's pose. Then she caught herself. "You're testing me," she said,
"that's schoolyard stuff." "Oh, no, I'm not," he said, "honest. But it's like
I love this without belief and you love it with belief, and one of us is miss-
ing something and it's got to be me. I just like all this stuff going on.
'Member the poem, 'We sit around in a ring and suppose. The secret sits in
the middle and knows?' So you know." "Why not the country club?" she
asked. "I've got a wicked slice," he said, "nobody wants to play with me.
I'm in the woods all the time with the poison ivy. And I'm immune. They

catch it just looking." "That's deep," she said. He giggled. "My slices go in a hundred yards. Somebody told me to use left-handed clubs. At least I'd land on another fairway."

The rabbi rose to go. "No, wait," he said, "it *is* deep, why I don't go there, but deep like just happiness, I'm happy here. I wouldn't be tomorrow. Tomorrow I'd have to be like a crocodile just to stay alive. So why are you happy here? You don't have to tell me." The rabbi stayed standing, leaning her hip against the bench in front. Which he saw as nice and round, and he blushed. "I don't want . . ." he said, and couldn't finish. She started to smile. "You like my look?" she asked. "You know I do," he said, "and I have the woman I want. But when you're up there and I hear everything coming out of a woman instead of a man, I feel at home in this world. I feel the wood better, and I am smelling my wife's powder, she very restrained, but I can pick it up when you work, I even notice the buttons on my coat. My wife changes my buttons. She finds these things, mother-of-pearl, amber, whalebone, I never know until you make me look." "Then you don't hear much of what I say," the rabbi said. "No," he said, "but I know your voice. I can taste it, like Earl Gray tea, smoky. I'm lost in this." "In what?" she asked. "In this," he waved his arm around, benches, reader's stand, torah scrolls, groups in shawls, visitors at doors, motion in the galleries upstairs. "This could go in a minute," she said, "it has gone in a minute, machine gun, molotov cocktail. Then what?" "Then nothing," he said, "unless we go somewhere."

He was now dead still and waiting, the way open space waits, for the appearance of a bird or a plume of smoke. She was blushing, with feeling, not embarrassment. "We go somewhere," she said. "Where?" he asked. "I can't tell you," she said, "I'm afraid to." "I'm too crude?" he asked. "No, you're a man," she said, "and where we go is a woman . . . no . . . like a woman . . . a belly . . . not for food . . . for . . . for pity . . . for seed, only seed is death, and it comes out life, and I'm afraid a man would . . . would think that's funny or crazy that sperm is death and egg is life, but I really mean a God who . . . " "Get's screwed?" the man asked. "Raped? And makes something? The fruit of rape?" His voice said this softly. Then even more softly, "Do you come from rape?" "I do," she said, "I'm Jewish from my mother." "Let me touch you," he said, "rub you off on me." "If you'll give me your tongue," she said. "Nobody hears it from me," he said. He put his hand on her belly, his palm. "You cure my slice?" he asked. "No," she said, "so you have to sit here on Sabbath." He dropped his hand. "Blood type O," he said, "suits everybody. I'm here." And she left. Her breasts like puppies. Her hip like a new moon.

10th Sunday, Ordinary Time

Loathly Lady Stuff

And so we have no eyes for things that
are visible, but only for things that
are invisible; for visible things last
only for a time, and the invisible
things are eternal.
　　　　—2 Corinthians 4:18

A woman was standing before a full length mirror. Looking at a scar. Hysterectomy scar that ran from her navel down to her hair. It was an old one but fresh in her memory, the bleeding before, the desert dryness after. And the distance from both men and women which had developed in the years that followed. "So, Eve," she said, "it was the apple after all, not your steamy sex." She stood a little longer. It was a ritual with her. She would not turn away from the mirror until she loved what she saw. The Loathly Lady stuff had to go first, knees like an elephant, toes like a turkey, crotch like Hitler, "Oh stop, stop, it's a map, a terrain map, touched by sun and moon and man and manchild, three sons that were carnivores and herbivores and omnivores, and their women were lions, harts and leaping does, and their babies sea otters, mix and match logical positivism, brrrr mind, flip off and leave the world to darkness and to me." Then she was calm and a sweet taste came to her tongue, she loved this terrain in the mirror and got back inside it as into a long gown.

Her husband wanted the bathroom. "D minus 15 and counting," he said through the door as he tugged at the bureau for some fresh shorts and sox. She turned the knob so the door opened a crack, then she backed so she saw herself at a slightly different angle. He pushed the door the rest of the way and stood there naked himself. "Ugh," he said, "me Tarzan." And he wagged his kind of big belly. She had been after him to do situps. He had, but got harder like a medicine ball, not flatter like a frisbee. "Gotta go, really," he said, "all that fruit last night. Did you ever taste such good mangos? Retreat, dear, retreat, save your troops." "I'll wear my bikini to Mass," she said as she slid past him and drew the door shut.

She went to the window where the morning breeze off the cove chilled her slightly, goose bumps, contraction of skin, and there was salt that bit slightly. "This is the last day of the world," she thought. There was someone on the dock down below to her right. Her cottage was on a promontory some thirty feet up. Someone standing on the last board with toes out over the water. The tide was high and ready to turn. She reached for her glasses on the night table and looked again. She saw a pregnant woman. Who edged out on that last plank a bit more, a slight teeter to the movement. Her nightgown made her look like a baloon spinnaker. She was going to drop into that water.

The woman in the bedroom shouted, "Steve, the dock!" and hit the door as she ran as on stilts for the stairs down to the porch out, then down the stone steps that curved in an S to meet another pathway that led to the dock. The other woman was gone off the end, under water but not far, her gown spread like a jelly fish, so the old woman could jump right in after and grab hold of the gown and pull her toward the dock and around to the ladder side, though the pregnant woman's head stayed under. Her husband came pounding awkwardly out the dock as naked as she and he reached down and grabbed the pregnant woman's head and pulled it up out of the water. But there seemed to be no breath. "Pull her along to the rocks," his wife said in an air-sucking breath. So he did, by the hair, his wife pushing. Then they both dragged her up between two of the rocks, scraping skin as they did on the shell crust.

"Hit her so she vomits," the wife said. "Hit her where?" the husband said. "Her back, then put her head down, then mouth to mouth." They knew they were guessing. So the man pounded a few times, got a dribble of water out of her mouth, then leaned her back so she lay across his lap and his wife could get her mouth on the woman's. They were wedged in between some rocks with their feet still in the water. The mouth to mouth worked and the pregnant woman began to breathe, then wretch some, breathe, then wretch the sea water she had swallowed, then try to stand in the unstable place. They got her on her feet and helped her up the few rocks left to the wood of the dock where she sat in her wet gown while the two stood above her until they could do something else. "Phone," the old woman said. But somebody else had seen what happened and they heard people up above halting in cars and jumping out and running down the path. The old woman sat behind the pregnant woman and just put her arms around her as if to rock her and the young woman yielded, let her head fall back on the old woman's shoulder.

A husband arrived, it was clear. "You crazy bitch," he shouted, pulling the old woman away and grabbing his wife under the armpits. "You know you can't swim. So you go falling in the water like a balloon and you sink like a rock. C'mon, teach you to swim, after the baby." It was rhetoric for the crowd. And it walled everyone out from doing anything. The husband tugged her through and up the path. "Your eyes'll fall out," he said to those looking. Then, in a private voice, "You crazy . . ." And they were gone.

"You're bleeding," the old man said to his woman. She looked down and saw she had scraped her belly on the rocks and there was a rash of blood drops from her navel to her hair, then down along one thigh to her knee. She looked up. "So are you," she said. Nobody seemed to notice them, everyone was looking up the path at the near naked form of a pregnant woman being hustled along by a near naked man in jockey shorts, being wrestled along. "And you're naked," she said. "Who says?" he said. And he enclosed her in his arms. "I thought you had your last child." "You'll just have to be more careful," she said, then, "Walk behind me, you'll scare the women." "Okay," he said, "and I won't have to catch cold." He put his hand on her shoulder and walked up the S shaped path behind her.

11th Sunday, Ordinary Time

The Thorns of Things

. . . I, the Lord, am the one who stunts
tall trees and makes the low ones grow,
who withers green trees and makes the
withered green.
  —Ezekiel 17:24

"I'll grow bigger 'n' hold him," the boy said to his mother. She was in the station wagon, the Irish setter in the back where the seats were lowered, and the dog was moving up and down with joy and anxiety because he had a ride. But his little master was not getting in. She had the window down as she talked to her son. "Somebody big will get him and later we'll get you another just like this one. He's knocking kids over, I told you, and their mommies and daddies are mad at us. Go in with your daddy and watch the baseball and I'll be back in a short while and make you a mini-pizza." The dog put his head right by her left ear, his nozzle and hanging tongue reaching for the boy. She pushed him back gently with her hand and he gave it a big lick and did a couple of turns from window to window wondering why everything was standing still. "So go in," she said.

He waited with his face crumbling, then bolted toward the back screen door, ran into the house, letting the screen slam behind him. His father was dozing, the sound down on the TV, strange, because his father knew everything about baseball, more than he knew about law, and that was a lot his mother told him. But his father sensed him and opened one eye for fun and did a fake snore, then closed the one and opened the other like an owl. Then he went into this huge writhe and yawn. That meant snake had just swallowed goat and was trying to get it down through detached jaws. But

130

the boy wasn't playing. He still wore his crumbled face. "*You* have what *you* want," he said. "He knocks you over," his father said. "He thumps you with his tail. He doesn't know and you can't explain to him. He needs a *big* master and *big* fields so he can chase birds and rabbits. I couldn't chain him in the backyard. So we let you grow and we get another one and he'll obey you because you're big. Okay?"

The boy felt helpless. He caught the sense. They had chained the dog and he had let him go and the dog was so happy he had knocked over the next door trash pails and little girls, the twins who looked like ice cream cones. "I go out back?" he asked. "Sure," his father said, "but not out of the yard, and look in on me every few minutes. Wake me up. This's a big game. You want to watch it with me? I'll tell you what's good." The boy shook his head. He turned and went out through the porch, down the stoop and across the backyard towards his mother's flowers.

She had the whole fence on three sides fronted with rose bushes. He went up to them wanting to be mean. He stood there thinking what to do. A scary bumble bee came right up to his nose looking to land. He was afraid to wave at it so he ducked, but it ducked with him. He backed and it backed with him. So he ran inside the screen door and it hovered outside deciding he was not a flower. Then it bombered away. He went back to the bushes. This time a butterfly, a white-winged one, and he let it land on his chest, but it left in crazy flight. And the roses were now unprotected. He reached for one, its stem, and pricked himself on some thorns. He had wanted to pull one off. Then he knew something that wasn't mean. Something for her. So she would understand. He took the stem again, this time with both hands and worked to break flower and stem off from the bush. He could feel the thorns cut into his hands and he started to cry a bit but he got a rose off, a nice one that started inside as almost white then got pink, even red, as it spread outward to its fringes. And it smelled like tea in his mother's special tin, the one with the egrets and marsh grass painted on it. He put it on the ground, then worked another one free from another bush, a red, red one. Then he did a white one. By this time there was a lot of blood on his hands and they were stinging.

He went and sat on the stoop holding the three flowers in his hurt hands. "You there?" his father said from just inside the kitchen. "Yup," he said. A can of beer hissed open. "She back?" "Nope," he said. "Want me to play frisbee?" "Nope," he said. He could hear steps. Then the screen door started to open. "Don't want to bang you," his father said. So he moved and let the door swing open. His father came down and sat beside him. And looked at what he was holding and the blood scratches. His father thought for a long time with the can of beer in his hands which were across his knees. "You want a little taste?" The boy shook his head. "You just want to wait?" The boy nodded. "Okay if I sit too?" The boy nodded.

The station wagon appeared in the driveway with one occupant now. It stopped near the stoop and his mother got out. She knew something was up. So she walked toward them saying nothing. The father just looked at his beer. The boy stood up and walked to her and reached the three flowers up. And she saw the blood scratches on his small hands. She took the flowers. "Do you want me to send the roses away? Because they scratch people? They don't chase people to scratch them." He started to cry. She squatted down in front of him and held the roses to her face to smell them. "Tea," she said. He nodded through the tears in his eyes. "You want me to get rid of these until you get bigger?" He shook his head no. "If they had legs and wanted to run, I couldn't keep them," she said. "Imagine a dog with thorns for a coat. You couldn't pat them. And the twins would be all scratched up next door." He said nothing. "So *I* get to keep what *I* want and *you* don't get to keep what *you* want?" He shook his head no. "Then what?" she asked. He didn't know. He just knew she had things that could hurt people and they were beautiful things and he liked the roses for the bumble bees though he had to run from them and the butterflies and the smell of tea where there wasn't any. "Love, listen," she said, "you'll grow into everything. It isn't all just this minute. There's a dog that will be born in a few years and it'll be your dog and you'll be tall then and so will the twins next door and that dog will heed you. And I have to judge. And your daddy." The boy didn't move. "Can I wash your hands so you don't get an infection?" He nodded.

She stood up, roses in one hand, and reached the other to take his. His father was still seated on the stoop. "You want me to hold them?" he asked, reaching for the flowers. She looked at the boy for an answer. He nodded. "Be right here," the father said as he moved aside to clear the door. "And am I starved! Ten minutes and I eat these. And I'll have a scratchy voice and kiss like tea." The boy beamed, back in the play world. "You eat 'em and *we* get all the pizza," the mother said. "I'm comin' and watch," the father said, "don't trust you guys." And the three went stomping into the house.

12th Sunday, Ordinary Time

For God's Sake!

Who pent up the sea behind closed doors
when it leapt tumultuous out of the
womb, when I wrapped it in a robe of
mist and made black clouds its swaddling
bands . . .?
                                    —Job 38:8

"It was an act of God, that wave, never saw anything like it, an' I been a fisherman thirty years. Took Sal right outa the wheelhouse and the glass and the doors. Lucky we had a lot of fish, brought us upright, this boat was on its beam. I burned myself on the diesel, like I fell in bed, and stuff hit me on the head from behind. Mario was afraid to come back from the bows so I got up to the wheel and got us around where we took the water right but there was no heading into it. So I swung around and ran with it, and Mario was looking at me out the bulkhead for when to run back and he could see better than I could what was catching us and I figured it was too big. But he ran like on roller skates, like a kid, and come in through the broken front and wanted to go back and look for Sal. He's my brother and Mario's his kid and we just fixed this boat. We had an old wooden one before and we figured a steel one would hold more. But if we had that wooden one we would have floated over what took him."

"So I had to hold Mario off, he was taking the wheel and begging me an' I had to shout 'Your father says no, for the love of God no!' it was Sal's words, he said 'for the love of God' because he was in a seminary for kids once and he didn't swear. And he meant that stuff. He used to go to church and get us blessed after Easter so we wouldn't sink. So Mario knew and he just looked at me so empty I nearly turned and we woulda followed Sal down. That water was going every which way, so we woke up

134

to staying afloat. 'Get the engine,' I says to Mario, and he catches it right away, it's a coffin down there, he's in it, but I'm on it an' going nowhere without him, so down he goes through this hatch we made so we could shout and keep the wheelhouse warm. And every time I turn and shout I see his curly head, his mother's, and I think maybe *I* shouldn't come home. *I* should be the one. My wife's gone, and we never had no kids, she couldn't, so who's to miss me. And that's when I saw a wave bigger, you just won't believe, and we caught the side of it, it seemed just to go around us, again like on roller skates, right at us, then around us. 'You playing, you bastard?' I shouted, and tip we go over on our beam again. And I hear Mario shout up, he's at the hatch, but he knows there's no jumping, 'You hold it?' he shouts, but he knows it's not muscle, it's eyes and it's luck, that sea is choosing. 'Yeah,' I shout, 'don't let that thing race.'"

"So he had to guess when the stern was out of the water, Jesus! It was just like rocking over a canyon, there'd be something, there'd be nothing, but he could feel it and he saved that engine. He played it like an organ in church. So that's how we found the eye of the thing and went with it as far as we could, then had to turn and take it on the bows so we would't get tossed onshore. And the sea didn't want us so we got through. But we run out of fuel and had to get towed in from where we were. Though we could have sailed it, in fact we did part way, Mario's smart, we kept some sail from the wooden boat, and he used our booms to spread some which took us kind of heavy, we didn't have the strength to dump the fish."

"Then the cutter came and took us in tow and I steered. But Mario, he stood on the stern and I think he wanted to walk right off it, run off it, back to see if Sal was afloat maybe. He's an imaginative kid, like me once, he could feel it, a head floating up and down thirty, forty feet, drinking salt and rain. So I hope Sal went straight down, oh I hope, and stays down, I hope, not floats like a bag of air. He loved this, the sea we fished, it was seminary still, and he never asked me what we made. He was just there when we were to go, his wife made him the best bed roll, and she put up food nothing could spoil, and he walked right away happy when we had the fish out. He was like a thirst for big things and stuck in this boat to see the big things."

"So I says to Mario, 'You don't come no more. She can't lose two. He's gonna break her heart and you can't break twice, you die on the second.' And he says, 'That doesn't happen but once, you won't see that wave again.' 'Like you won't see Sal again,' I says, and he says, 'I will see him. I saw him and I couldn't tell you, I saw his head, it was way over us when we righted. He was in that wave and we were swung around. I couldn't get back to you when you reached the wheel.' 'But I put no lie on him,' I says, 'for God's sake don't, he meant.' And Mario just put his arms around me like it was Sal, and he's just this minute gone. I told him I'd tell you, Sarge, he's got to tell her. So you write it's an act of God and take a look at that wheelhouse, and you tell me. And we wear jackets when we don't work, lower insurance, and they'd float a horse, but I only hope he pulled the string or he was knocked out or I see him too floating forever up and down until they eat him like we eat them. So if you don't mind I gotta get this fish out and, Jesus, the dead fish make it home. . . I'll come down and sign that after at the station, okay?"

The Devil's Envy

It was the devil's envy that brought
death into the world, as those who are
his partners will discover.
—Wisdom 2:24

"I bury people cheaply," a woman said to the chair's question, "that's why I get the city's business. What happens to the bill after I send it is not under my control."

"You're saying the bill is padded after you send it in?" the chair continued.

"I say I bury the city's corpses cheaply, that's all I say, and the city pays me for what I bill, that's all I say. You have my records. If there's a problem, it's on your side not mine." "I'm looking at a fashion model woman," the chair continued as if not hearing the testimony given, "she says she's an undertaker who does city business at low cost, and a lot of it, and my mind has a red alert on, something doesn't square, low bills submitted, high bills paid, low records from you, high records from the city. Somebody else should be well dressed."

"I have declared my wealth to you," the woman said. "I had an IRS audit done. Never mind what I look like. Ask me questions that solve a real problem or let me go, I'm not wind for your flag to flap in."

"Don't take that tone with this committee, Madame Undertaker, your industry is often a questionable one. And you're not Joan of Arc."

"And I'm not a Salem witch either, Mr. Chairman. And question my industry if you want to. I can handle it. Handling a fog machine is something different. It's you who can't believe that a contract can be won on quality. That's why you think the crookedness must be with me."

"Well tell me about you and your quality," the chair said, "point me in the right direction." The woman said nothing. Neither did the chair. "You going to take the fifth?" the chair asked.

"No," she answered, "nor am I going to take any bullshit. I'll instruct the ignorant, but not the arrogant."

"Instruct the ignorant," the chair said, "that's Catholic catechism, isn't it?"

"Right," she answered. "So is bury the dead."

"Ah," he said, "the corporal works of mercy. You in this as a work of mercy? Mercy pays."

"Ignorance does too," she said.

"Okay, Madame Undertaker, instruct my ignorance. What's a nice girl like you doing in a business like this?"

"Just tell me why you ask?" the woman said. "Tell me what this has got to do with padded records?"

"I need to get to that," the chair said, "I need to turn off the red light in my mind that says a fine looking woman can't be an undertaker, can't make her living at it. If I get beyond that I can ask what do you think happened to those bills. We pay for a lot of stiffs to be buried."

"I don't have to do this, but I will," the woman said, "and it will take a little history."

"Okay," the chair said, "we have time."

"I don't need time," she answered, "I need mind."

"Mind, then," the chair said.

"My father," the woman said, "he was drafted in World War II. He worked in a drugstore so they put him in the medics. In the medics he was put in charge of the dead, burying them, shipping them home. So he was given one concentration camp after the war to clean up. Then he was in charge of reburial and later graves identification. So when he came back and married in the late forties, he had a skill. He worked for the city, in the morgue, for some ten years. He had a breakdown when I was a little girl because he saw too much death, had to handle too much of it. But he worked it through. And it was religion that did it. A sense that life was not wasted. But nothing in the funeral business really showed that. Taps and flags were stupid, he thought. Real dignity was not. And the problem was the living as much as the dead. So he started a funeral business. And he bought that old church in the South End. So people could be waked in a church. And he read about those old societies in Rome that buried paupers in the most dignified way possible, *Bona Mors* societies that paid all the costs. Humans are not trash. He had one child, my father, he wanted a boy to carry on, but he had me, and he made sense to me. So when he died, I took over the "business" as you call it. I became a mortician. He had a lot of contacts with the city. So he was given derelicts to bury. Because he would make the death of a bum look dignified, and officials could gain political clout pretending they were the ones who insisted on it. Now this matter of double billing shows up. And the real dead are the ones with their pockets lined. I dress bright now because I have to dress dull almost every night. But I am not in the trash business, Mr. Chairman, some of your city people are. And if you confuse me with them, I'm going to go after your political hide, something I've never done before. I belong to a *Bona Mors* society too. And you will put no bad name on it." She stopped.

"I'm not scared," the chair said, "and the red light is still flickering a bit. You're too beautiful for the job."

"Ah," the woman said, "I should be out breeding not burying, or seeing a shrink to get my kicks back straight, necrophilia? You want me to bring in my husband? I had to force him to stay away. He's a lawyer and he wanted to be my counsel and tie you up in knots. He went to school with you but you won't remember. Parochial school's a long way back. But I said to him the truth's enough, and Mr. Chairman will get the truth."

"Okay, the truth, you told me," the chair said, "but how come these bills can get padded and nobody know except by accident when you bury a bum who's really the son of a historic figure? So they come and thank you and offer to pay. You tell them to pay the city x and the city says no it cost y. And the newspapers go on a binge. I won't have any hide left, Madame Undertaker, for you or anyone else to have if I don't find who creamed off the corpses."

"We both understand now," the woman said, "that it's my policy that makes this possible. No one can pad a padded bill. And there's no trace of kickback to me. No trace because there isn't any kickback. So you need to find someone on your side of this whose chances for fraud are less than anyone else's. So someone from the poorer wards and someone in the treasurer's office who can fake bills. There are a lot of dead on the poorer streets, and a lot of dead out of City Hospital. But the neatest way is this. Otherwise there are too many intermediate palms to tickle and too many snail tracks."

"You sure you're just an undertaker?" the chair asked. "If you know all this now, you could have known it yesterday, could have known your low price would be exploited!"

"Once again," the woman answered, "you think I should do what everyone else does. I should live the life of a pretty woman. And give no one a chance for fraud. Charge high prices to bury bums. Okay, I'll offer you a package deal. Let me be your undertaker. I'll do you for half price, your wife for three quarters, any children below ten for cost, babies for nothing, sons and daughters three quarters, just so long as I get the whole family. You've got a big one. And I'll come out with a good profit. That profit will let me bury all the city bums I get at a low price, and do it with as much dignity as I do you, though you may want more pomp, I mean priests and sopranos and a bank of flowers. And I'll get some nice clothes out of it and good schools for my two kids. And it'll be legit and scrutinized by the IRS. So what do you say?"

"This is no place to make a deal about death," the chair said.

"Deals about death are what you are investigating," she said. He looked at her somewhat stunned. "So treating someone as a human being *is* the issue, isn't it?" she asked. "Anything else and we are arguing about trash disposal." She waited, then said, "You are only interested in the money. You follow the money." She waited again. Then she said, "Not the trash."

Madness In, Madness Out

We are filled with contempt./Indeed
all too full is our soul with the
scorn of the rich,/with the proud
man's disdain.
—Psalm 123:3-4

"What you do not understand is that we win by driving them mad," the leader said. "Everybody thinks we think only in the short term. We are holding you hostage for what? So we can swap you for someone who is now useless to us? No. You feel your own rage? Your own futility? Now multiply that. By hundreds of millions. Now take away from hundreds of millions the power to do anything about you. Yes. You come from a civilized country. Its civilization makes it powerless in this matter.

And your good friends in the south. We force them to kill day in and day out, women and children included. Do you see the madness we are inducing? They blamed us for killing a girl. They examined her body. The bullet in it was their own bullet. Their rage is now split. Like a schizophrenia. The more this happens, the more they kill, the more their dream of a land of their own becomes a nightmare. Until they are again at the absolute point where their good is satanic and their evil is angelic. Exactly as back in Europe after the Holocaust. Only this time God has not set them up as victims, the godless have, the world of goodness without God has. The world of justice and truth has, set them up as victims. But not of ovens. Of their own souls. Their own souls go mad, but not quite all the way. Some part is still aware of the deception, and that intensifies the madness. So you see why we practice "suicide" as you call it, madness. We know the madness, and how to live in it, and how to use it, but they do not.

So we move out of madness as they move into it. Then we shall take care of them."

The leader stopped speaking. He was wearing a stocking mask, but had no weapon. His guards had the weapons. The hostage seated on the bed was blank. He did not respond to what he just heard. He loosened another button on his shirt. The extra men in his cell-like room made the air closer.

"I'm telling you this," the leader continued, "because the stupidity of your people has made me impatient. Your people think we are cunning only the way animals are cunning. Not the way human beings are. So I have decided to have mercy on them. And tell them what is happening to them. Once they are aware they are being led into madness they will respect us and will become fearful and withdraw support from the south in order to stay sane and enjoy the goods of life until life is naturally over and everything ceases for them."

The hostage on the cot still looked blank. He smoothed the bedspread on either side of him, slowly, as if doing it unconsciously.

"So I'm letting you go," the leader continued. "You know what I have said to you is true. You know it makes sense. You will tell your people this. And your people's friends to the south. We will make them mad." The hostage reacted in no way. "You told me he was clear," the leader muttered to his guards. "He was clear," a guard said. "Last night we showed him new photos of his wife and family. He was happy. This may be a reaction. To protect himself against hope."

"I'm clear," the hostage said, smoothing his jeans a bit, but with the same distracted stroke. "It's you who are not." He then looked at the leader seated in a chair opposite the bed. The leader made a helpless gesture with his hands, as if after a wasted effort. "They love being crazy," the hostage said. "You are driving them into something they love. Craziness forgives anything. As it does for you. You are driving them to be you." The hostage felt a hardening of mood in the room.

The leader sensed it too, his guards were not as smart as he thought. And he had to recover them. "No, not like us," he said. "God is with us whatever we do. God is with you only if you do things right. And you have to have God with you. Even when you are crazy." The hardening in the guards softened. "God is with us whatever we do," the leader repeated.

Then he waited as if waiting to spring a trap. The hostage was now looking at him with great calmness. "You are right," the hostage said, "even the fanatics to the south are afraid of judgment." The leader relaxed more. "So you will go," he said, "and you will tell them they are dealing with cunning. It is not animal. It is more than they can match."

"I do not understand why you are being merciful to them," the hostage said. "Unless you cannot abide being treated as an animal. A mad dog that can only be shot. Whose God is even a madder dog." There was a quick cocking of guns, the leader had to spread both hands, and they were menacing hands for all that he had no weapons. There was a sacredness to his being so he was surely a clan leader, not a recruit from an ad hoc group. He was enraged and fighting for self control. "So if you let me go," the hostage continued, "I will convince them that you are mad dogs and your God an even madder one." There was a shot, but it was knocked wide of the hostage, one guard controlling another, but the bullet hacked out a hunk of cinder block just behind the hostage's head.

"You are asking for death," the leader said. "No," the hostage said. "And I am not asking for life either. I am not asking you for anything. You can make me ask, that is sure, enough pain will make anyone ask for anything. Or almost anyone. There are some people who can stand hell and still spit defiance. I am not one of them." He waited, almost respectfully, respectful of the conversation.

"We took you because your mind worked," the leader said, "but it does not. You know we are not dogs. Yet you would say so. To justify what you would do to us. You will not tell them the truth of what we are doing." He paused. "You do see it, though." Then, "You do not want to save your people." Then, "Nor do you want to save mine." The hostage felt the pressure.

"You don't have to prove you can drive me crazy," he said to the leader. "But I can tell you a story. The one man who sees the truth when no one else does is the one man who is crazy."

"We will simply make you disappear," the leader said as he rose to go. "No one will know anything, they will live in hope for you, and they will treat us with care lest you be harmed. You are only good as nothing."

"You are a dog, and your God is a dog," the hostage said fiercely.

The shots caught him across the midriff and lifted him still seated back against the wall, then the spray shattered the ceiling as someone knocked the firing gun up in the air, too late to save the hostage. Then the firing stopped. The leader was trembling with rage. "Hold him!" he said, and two guards grabbed the third who had fired. "A gun!" the leader said. He was handed one. He shot the offending guard right in the chest even as he was being held by his fellow guards. And they flinched with anger and fear and let the body drop and looked at the leader with rebellion surging into their faces. He shot quickly two more times and the guards went down. The door behind him was kicked open and there was a corridor full of armed men outside it.

"They were traitors," the leader said as he came and stood in the doorway. "God has punished them." And he walked through the lowering guns towards the exit where outside the rest of his people waited.

Lady Samson

*Go away, seer; get back to the land of
Judah . . . we want no more prophesying
in Bethel; this is the royal sanctuary,
the national temple.*
—Amos 7:12-13

"The truth is useless," a man was saying to a woman, "and you telling it even more useless." They had finished dinner, in a noisy Deli-Bar, gourmet food kind, small tables, so closeness despite the bustle of the place. Hard to overhear much or get picked out. She looked wounded even more by what he said. She hadn't touched her seafood salad. Nor her glass of wine. "You've already been isolated," the man continued. "The action has shifted to other channels. The witch hunt you'd start if you talked would be like a fight in the stands."

"I know someone caused a death," she said. Her voice was monotone. "A woman's death. To scare a man. A man who knew our treachery. But one we could still use. If we showed him he was next. So cooperate."

"You don't know her," he said, "you don't know him. You just pieced this together from what came over your desk."

"I do know her," the woman said, "she did the watercolors of jungle birds her embassy showed. Oh, they were so intense, but so like zen paintings, ready to vanish if you tried to hold them."

"Look," he said, "I'm honestly not trying to keep you for myself. Or keep you clean so I can go on with my life. I'm really cynical. And I know that in this case the truth will do no good. If they ever get wind of what you know you'll be out quick. Or if you're not, they'll make hash out of you for that time you were in St. Elizabeth's. Once you break, you're always broken. And no new laws will be made to stop this covert stuff."

"So, it's my next attempt at suicide?" she asked.

"Yes," he said, "and I'd let you do it if you brought their house down, Lady Samson, but you won't."

"They really use drug money," she blurted, "and they feed it to conservative missionaries. Who love the good they can do. So no native says a peep with a mouthful of bread. 'Where the poppies grow/beneath the crosses row on row.'"

"Yes, yes, yes," he said softly, "so no, no, no. Some evil you have to leave to God."

"They will know I saw that data," she said, "the desks it goes to are noted."

"But he's the last one to get the data, isn't he?" the man asked.

"Yes," she said.

"And he hasn't touched you?"

"No," she said, "I think he likes me. The red hair. Even the freckles. He feels raw and untamed. A lot of men do with redheads." She was almost talking to herself. "And a woman's no real threat. Loss of job maybe. But he gets a reputation as a stud. Talk circuit then to kids in college who like broken eggs. Damage, but no harm."

"But you're somewhere else," he said, "the great God truth has got you."

She flushed a bit. "Be cynical," she said, "but not mean."

He looked down at his plate. Seafood salad too. He had taken the lobster bits and left the scallops which were like dead eyes. "I just think the cause of all things should pay the price of all things."

"Don't love me too much," she said. "I need you cold and clear. What you said earlier makes some sense. I'm almost absolved. No good can come from the truth if I tell it."

He was staring at her now, raw and untamed, his clarity gone. "Broken eggs," he said, "take a good look at some." He waited, then said, "I just know they'll kill you or drive you crazy."

"Then you'll be where I am," she said, "talking to someone saying what shall I do with what I know. Then that someone will be where you were, talking to someone else saying what shall I do." He couldn't respond. "In fact," she continued, "maybe I've killed you. This is an obscure place, but we're talking and not really eating and anyone with two eyes in their heads . . ."

"Okay," he said, "then blow the whistle from here. That pay phone at the end of the bar. The Post will listen. So you won't die. I'll have to watch you break." His lips were quivering. He bit them. He left teeth marks.

"I can't," she said, and said calmly. "There's been someone on that phone for the last twenty minutes. And will stay on it."

"Is there a bar phone?" the man asked, not looking.

"Bartender's on it, washing dishes at the same time," she answered.

"He's the only one?"

"No," she said, "the other one is doing all the drinks."

"So they do know," he said.

"Yes," she said. "They left me alone while I was deciding. They're telling him now he can't have his redhead."

"I have a butane lighter on me," he said. "If I open its nozzle it shoots fire. I sometimes use it to start kindling in the woods. I'll go line up for a phone call and I'll light that guy's coat on fire. Like the flames scared me and I threw it from me. I'll grab the extinguisher right beside the kitchen IN door and spray him. You run to help. Slide behind him, cut off his call, and dial yourself the Post. The bartender will have to stop and call the Fire Dept. You'll have five minutes to tell the Post. Identify yourself fully first, they record, then say you want to blow a whistle, on whom, and what your evidence is, and you may not make it down to them, but if you can you will. And if you're killed, they should follow your killing to the source. Okay?"

"Okay," she said.

"And the bartender?"

"Still on," she said.

"I never did anything criminal before," he said, "and make it look good."

"Maybe you shouldn't," she said, "he might be burned."

"His burns will heal."

"We're crazy already," she said.

"We can heal that too," he said. "You set? I'll light my cigarette, the whoosh will scare me, I'll toss it on him, grab the extinguisher, spray him, you run to me, then slide to the phone."

"He'll know what you're doing," she said.

"When I do it," he said.

"Don't," she said, "don't, don't." Her voice became weaker as she said this. Her head started to bend towards her plate. Then halted as she regained control. She lifted it and it looked drained of blood almost completely. She rose and left the table and walked to the bar and he followed her. She reached over the bar and took the phone off the bartender's shoulder, her hand shaking. "I need to phone for some insulin, I've an attack coming and soon." People at the bar heard her. He surrendered the phone uneasily to this blanched and shaking woman, then the dialing part. She turned her back to him and sank to the floor between the stools, the phone in her lap, and drew her knees up so her legs showed, then bent into the mouthpiece, dialed Information, got the Post's number, all in a fumbling manner. Then she dialed the Post and spoke into the phone from her huddle on the ground. Her man was kneeling in front of her, turning every now and then to say, "She forgot her medicine. It'll be okay." She hung up. "They'll come and get me," she said. She handed off the phone and started to get up.

There were two shots. One caught her and killed her. The other caught the bartender and killed him. The pay phone was dangling off its hook. And the man who had used it went crashing through the crowd, out the door and into a waiting cab. The survivor had only hearsay evidence. And nowhere to go with it.

16th Sunday, Ordinary Time

The Kiss of the Cross

Doom for the shepherds who allow
the flock of my pasture to be de-
stroyed and scattered—it is the
Lord who speaks!
　　　　—Jeremiah 23:1

"I'm one of those Indians," an old man was saying, "high steel Indians. I shake now, but that's from something else. I built the Empire State building." He was talking to a priest, a new one, up to the reservation from St. Louis, a photographer also, art photography. He was doing the old men because not many Indian men lived to be old, and there was often a story of survival. "I have a picture of me when we put the tree on top of it. And another when I dropped my pants and mooned at all of New York. But nobody saw except this Cherokee with the brownie camera, and he laughed so he dropped the camera, but it landed in one of those nets that caught the rivets if a guy missed catching one in those funnel buckets they had. Those guys better not miss or they got a hot foot in their shirt pockets. So we picked up the camera and the picture was okay. You want it instead? Or the tree one? You won't have to waste film."

"I want you now," the priest said, cradling his Haselblad camera in his lap. It was hung from his neck on an Indian wampum belt.

"I'm just a shaking tree now," the Indian said. "I used to be steel with steel. You missed me. It's like you take a picture of a horse print and the horse is long gone."

"There aren't many horse prints left," the priest said. "And if I can make a show at the school maybe some young guys won't want to drink themselves to death. They may want to see what happens in the long years."

149

"I used to drink, outside jobs," the Indian said. "Never during. I had to go get somebody once. He drank during. He was up on a girder. We were at sixty stories. I mean a straight up girder and he was waiting for a crossbeam to come in. He got dizzy for the first time. He was squatting there and puking too, so I wasn't going to go up a slippery steel. I got on a crane hook and had the crane lift me in behind the guy and I grab him by his belt in back so he can't grab me and he was kicking and clawing but I had him like a lobster so the crane guy dropped us fast all the way down to the net and he slowed us just right so I let the other guy go and he hit the net easy. But that's steel mesh so he got scraped. Then I had the crane guy swing me back up and put me where the other guy had been and it was pukey so I peed on it. You wouldn't believe. Just had enough to wash the top. Then I got on it off the hook and waited until they brought up the crossbeam. So I would never drink on a job. I used to go to movies and root for the Indians. Sometimes get kicked out, but I'd go to another one and let out war whoops. Then I'd fight with the manager and tell him the Indians were the good guys. Met a lot of nice managers. They'd take me in the projection booths and show me. But I got drunk after the Empire State. Somebody found me in Central Park. I had nothing left. So I had to get another job. Went on like that until the War."

"So you were just lucky," the priest said, sounding a little disappointed. "It's like the young will last only if they're lucky."

"No, I saw God," the old Indian said, "but that still will not help. Unless you can take a picture of the spirit inside."

"Can't," said the priest, "but some people think I can and are afraid I'll steal it, their spirit, and they'll be empty, like shucks of corn."

"You're not interested in my spirit?" the old Indian asked.

"I am," said the priest, and sat back to listen. "You interested in God too?" the Indian asked. "Well, yes," the priest said.

"I was put in the paratroops," the Indian said. "Army figured I'd jump even without a chute. It was all for invading Europe. And we copied the Germans. But I was night drops, so we had to learn on black chutes with blackened faces and jump into tall trees so if we caught we'd work ourselves loose instead of hanging there like meat. So I went into Normandy at night and I caught on the steeple of a church and I was dead if I didn't move. It was like a tall thin teepee and the cross had caught the chute. And the cross was on a weathervane of a fish, like below it, like the pedals of an air pump for those old automobiles. So I cut the shoulder straps with my knife and hung by my hands. I couldn't get rid of all my junk at first. I had to go up silk. I held on with my teeth too. And the steeple was slate. If that silk ever ripped. So I got to the top. And I saw I had to pull the chute up because there were searchlights from German cars. I stood on the weathervane, and the cross came up to my crotch. And they were anchored well enough. I stood like a saint. I figured no one would believe it, a man standing on the point of a steeple during a shootout. I hoped the Germans were new to the town. And a couple of lights did skin by me. But I stood like a saint I had seen in church here, my eyes up to the heavens, my hands on my breast. And the lights skinned by. And the shooting. I knew my guys were getting it. So near dawn I had to use the chute again. I slit it more with my knife and made a knotted rope of it. And the cross and the fish held. And the chute was long enough so I could drop onto the rooftree of the church. So I kissed the cross thanks before I lowered. It was iron. But I kissed flesh. And it wasn't my own. And I saw a face. And I saw cheeks. With a mark from my mouth on it. And I was Judas. And I knew why. The cross smelled like that girder I pulled the guy off, like drink and puke. Then the face went. It was the only time that face could talk to me. No place else would I see it. So I got down. Broke in a window in the steeple. And down into the church. I never drank again. I worked a lot of steel. Until the shake came. Then I came home. You see the cross on my face?"

"No," the priest said.

"It's there," the Indian said. "I feel it, every minute I feel it. But I don't see the face anymore." "Do you want to?" the priest asked. "Yes," the Indian said. "I want to know if I didn't kill him again." The priest hefted his Haselbald a bit. There was nothing quick and easy to say. "You tell this to people?" he asked. "Lots of people," the Indian said. "They think I'm cracked. They think the liquor did it before I stopped. And the war did the rest."

"Maybe if it was one of your ancestors who appeared," the priest said. "My ancestors do not live there," the Indian said. "They do not know high steel or drink or war from the air. That is why I shake." The priest waited for more in perfect stillness. "They come to me," the Indian went on, "and ask me to explain. I try but they do not understand. They say they are going to die if they do not understand. They are going to die. And I am Judas again. If you could photo the cross on my face, I could send Jesus to them and he would explain to them, and they could explain to the young . . ."

"I cannot," the priest said.

"Then take these," the Indian said. "This is me holding the tree at the top of the Empire State building, and this is me mooning at New York City. They may help."

17th Sunday, Ordinary Time

Ticket Crisis

I, the prisoner in the Lord, im-
plore you to lead a life worthy
of your vocation.
—Ephesians 4:1

She loved to make bread. On Saturdays. The travel agency could fly, she'd work for them Monday through Friday, not one more minute. She was good, so they accepted. And her family could go fly too. She did the suppers all week for two teenage maws and one white, male caucasian, Smith-Barney type earning money the old fashioned way, plod, plod, munch, munch. These words were in her head as she kneaded the dough, sprinkled the flour, kneaded it more, then patted it into a round shape and fitted it into a rectangular pan, the last of six loaves. The family would eat one, reluctantly. She'd eat a second. And four would go to a People's Park kitchen. She'd seen how the People wolfed it down, sometimes spat it out, there was too much taste to it. They wanted gum bread that turned into a wad of wet paper in their mouths. She put the six bread pans into the oven, set the temperature, and began to clean up, the egg shells, the scatterings of flour, the bits of dough, the bowls, she enjoyed this too, enormously, sloshing the water around, scraping the kneading board, no computer blips, times, dates, prices, penalties. So that was done.

The phone rang. The Agency. "There's someone here who says you did her ticket and it's all wrong." "Tell her to see me on Monday. I don't do tickets all wrong. She must have changed her mind." "Hang on a sec." It was the Agency owner speaking. He often took the Saturdays. Then he was back and the woman could hear an enraged voice in the background. "She says you did it all wrong," he said. "Then fix it," the woman said, "fix it to exactly what she wants." "I would like to," he said, "but she says

153

you should do it, she leaves tonight, and we should give her the ticket free, or she sues for loss of business." "She's crazy," the woman said to her boss, "tell her to sue." "Please come down," he asked. She thought. The bread aroma began to fill the kitchen softly. The teenaged maws would be home by twelve thirty, and plod, plod, munch, munch was already shaving upstairs before breakfast. "You want me to call the police before I come?" she asked. "No," he said. "Ten minutes, okay?" "Ten minutes," she said.

She hung up, went to the head of the stairs, shouted up to him, "Ticket crisis, have to go!" The door opened. "Can't hear!" he said. "Office crisis, have to go down, be back at one, there's some quiche in the fridge, and the coffee's near fresh." "Okay," he said, or sang it like a basso buffo, he was a buffo in the buff on Saturdays. She had to tell him the girls were around. Then he would go into a huddle like Michelangelo's damned man in the Last Judgment and scurry knockneed behind a closed door. She tapped the oven lightly as she headed for the back. "Oh, don't nobody slam or down you go to matzah bread." She eased out, got in her car and was at the Agency in ten minutes.

She recognised the client as she walked in. A fidgety type who wanted to do Oran first, Istanbul second, Cairo third, then Damascus, then home. A strange itinerary to start with, lots of doubling back. So the woman had booked her to Madrid on TWA, then on Egypt Air to the other places. The client stood up when she entered. Like a rooster ready to fly. "You have me running all over the stupid sky," she shouted, and she flung the ticket on the woman agent's desk. "Now you straighten this out. And you pay the penalty." The agent sat at her desk, started her computer, brought up the ticket and itinerary as the client stood there breathing rage. The computer showed the agent that the ticket was exactly what the client asked for. So she leaned back from her screen and desk and looked at the client. "What's the game?" she asked. The rage turned to a white-faced hatred. "I told you I wanted Istanbul, Damascus, Cairo, Oran. You scrambled this because you don't know the one from the other. Now you set it right. And learn. That is why I insisted you come here. It is no good for him to learn." And she pointed to the boss.

"This ticket is exactly what you asked for," the agent said. "Then you give me my money back!" the client said. "And I will get someone to do it right." "You get your money back less the penalty of twenty-five per cent," the agent said. "You asked for a fixed date ticket and you got it. Any changes and you lose. I told you." The client reached down on the agent's desk and grabbed the ticket, then backed towards the door. She held the ticket up in her hand like a warrant. "This will come back on you," she said.

"Wait," the agent said. The client stood there. The agent went from behind her desk towards the client at the door. She took the ticket and led the client back towards her desk. "Tell me the order of cities again," she said. The client sat in the chair like someone exhausted from emotion. She spoke slowly to the agent. "Istanbul first, Damascus second, Cairo third, then Oran. And home through Madrid." "Okay," said the agent. It took twenty minutes to work out the changes. Then the agent hit the button for print and in the back room the printer did the ticket. She went in and handed it to the client. "We pay the penalty," she said. The client went very quietly to the door, opened it and left.

Her boss was already dialing. It took him fifteen minutes to explain it to the local Bureau. Then he hung up. The woman still sat at her desk, her computer on, the new itinerary still bold on the screen. "She told us the only way she could permit herself," she said. "She'll never come back from Madrid. But that ticket will. And we catch whoever's on it." She pressed save and then turned off her machine. "She could have come to you quietly," the woman continued to her boss. "Said she had simply gotten confused. Paid the twenty-five percent." He nodded. "Walked out that door and given some monster a good cover in woman's clothes." She got up. "I've bread baking." He nodded. "That's better," he said. "No," the woman said, "not these days."

Spooky Stuff

He who believes in me will never thirst.
—John 6:35

"We used to be giants," the bellhop said. "Hee, hee. The old people found mammoth bones, thought they were human. So we shrank because we did wrong, they said. Now we are fat chickens without feathers. You're a mammoth." He was talking to a very tall gringo who had just asked him were the Zocalo was and gotten directions. The bellhop was seventy, he said, but really eighty. The hotel kept him because he could speak English and give directions to its few American tourists. Most were finicky, didn't like taking showers in the same stall with some harmless snails. So they stayed at little Americas instead of little Mexicos.

"You don't fit in the bed," the bellhop continued. He had thick glasses he didn't wash so they looked clouded. And his uniform coat was a button out of whack which made his collar higher on one side than the other. "No," said the tall gringo, "but I've learned to sleep like a jacknife." "You'll be born again that way," the old man said. "Down in Yucatan the old people buried their babies like jacknifes, but inside a pot like a woman, so they would come back in an earthquake and be alive. Hee, hee, and be scared crazy by the buses. You watch out for buses, they belch and you get black lung." "How do you know about black lung?" the tall man asked. "I read it once," the old man said. "I could read. I was in school once. Up in Texas. I was in jail and teachers came sometimes. So I read newspapers until I got out." "What were you in jail for?" the tall man asked. He had a fistful of travel maps in his hand and was sorting through them to get a street map of the city. He had a shoulder bag to stuff them in. "I stole a train, hee, hee," the old man said.

He reached behind him to press the elevator button for a guest. That was his station, by the elevator, to answer questions, not to lug bags. "Just stole a train?" the tall man said, grinning a bit. "That doesn't really seem like much. No place to hide it and you can't eat it." "We ate it," the old man said, "hee, hee, we ate it empty." The tall man looked puzzled. "There was beans and soup and pineapple, two carloads, still hooked to the engine. And we were out in a place along the line for Mexes. We did the road beds. And they fed us old cows, ones that died on them. So I go back with the rail car and pretend I'm going home. I look around and I see them break up a train and leave the engine with two box cars. I go over and ask a guy what's on. He kicks me away and says if I touch anything I get my crogies crushed. I know it must be food because he thinks I can smell food through wood and tin. Hee, hee, I was so hungry I bet I did. So I slouch away like a dog he's beaten. Then I run around the engine. The driver and his other man are out getting something like coffee and donuts. So I get on and I read brake and throttle. Then I drive the train right out of the yard and it goes back toward the camp where we were. And I brake there and I shout food! and they all come and we hack the cans open with our knives and we eat like the last day. So they catch me because they know who I am. I do five years and they kick me back here and keep my name on a list. If I go back I do five years more." But I do go back, hee, hee, I walk all over Texas. I help a cop one day fix a tire on his wagon. I was in a field eating tomatoes and he thought I worked. I just walked and I ate, enough to keep walking. Some of Texas is beautiful. Then I hitch on trucks and I even hitched on trains. But I start to go blind so I have to come back home." "Too bad," the tall man said, "there's a lot more to see." And he started to put his travel maps away.

"I see up close," the old man said, "like you, mammoth. Like my plate, but I feed like a hog, hee, hee, I mean my nose has to get close, then my glasses get steamed, so I don't know except by my nose. You want to know some other places to go? I tell you. Holy places. The rest is crap or a trap, hee, hee." "How would you know holy places?" the tall man asked, maybe with a little cruelty, and he moved a bit to leave. "It's where you trust someone with your life," the old man said. "Everything else is crap or a trap." "Then there's no holy place," the tall man said. "There's one anyway," the old man said. "I picked up a dog in Texas once. He picked me up. We walked a long time. This night a man came with a gun, he saw me in his field, just beans which grow in millions, and he could shoot me and nobody'd know. The dog went for him after the first shot. First shot caught me some in the arm. Second shot caught the dog, but I ran so the next shots were for the air. The man dragged the dog out in the road for the birds. But I went back and I buried the dog under the beans. Put all the beans back right. Someone ate brave dog later and didn't know. So one holy place. Then I find more where someone dies so someone lives. I tell you them sometime. Not now. I keep you from your visits."

"So," the tall man said, "out of the hotel, then left, then five blocks, then right five and that's the Zocalo." "Yes," the old man said, "you will smell the blood just before you get there. Just wave your hand in front of your face and it will go away. The blood is for us to care for, not for you, you are a tourist, we are Aztecs or what's left of them." "You lost me," the tall man said, and not as if he wanted a further explanation. "We have to drink it," the old man went on. "You smell a bowl of it placed under your nose. It is not for you. We drink it then someone has some life back until we digest, then they go back in the bowl again until someone else drinks." "You like spooky stuff," the tall man said. "I'll be one soon," the old man said, "hee, hee, and don't drink the water, it's spooky too."

19th Sunday, Ordinary Time

A Slice of Life

Try, then, to imitate God, as children
of his that he loves, and follow Christ
by loving as he loved, giving himself up
in our place as a fragrant offering. . .
—Ephesians 4:32, 5:2

"Yeah, well, we need you guys." A man said this to two priests. They were all at a fund raiser for a mayoral candidate. The man speaking had run twice on a get tough platform and had lost. He had sounded more like the thugs he wanted to stop than the nice guys he wanted to help. A lot of people were at the party. Tables of crayfish and jumbalaya and shrimp with pitchers of local beer. The two priests ran a labor school so they were interested in a reform choice.

"It's one thing to have to go fight. That means guys like me. Another thing to save home base. That means guys like you." He had a raw voice, an open jacket, a flat belly, though he drank, and beer. "When we were on Guadalcanal we had a good padre, he wanted to get to the guys when they were hit, but we told him no, we'll bring 'em back to you, lose one of us and it's nothin', lose one of you and there's no one for a month. And we didn't need help cuttin' enemy throats." He took a drink. "Couldn't kill those bastards with a bullet, had to go right into the cave with a knife. No room for anything else." He spread his legs as he spoke, as if to ease pressure on his groin. "But that padre wouldn't listen, until he saw me draggin' out a few cut throats and dumping them for body count. He got sick lookin', so I told him again, and he went back. You're just for our guys, I said, these guys are goin' somewhere else." He took another swallow. "So you stay inside those collars, make sure we end up in the right place, wouldn't want to meet those throats I cut in the wrong place and have to do

159

it all over again. Though geez I would, some things you gotta cut and you gotta have guys like me to do it, but if I came home to a protest like those 'Nam guys, I woulda kept my knife and made a few sopranos, they had the hair already, so they'd just have to wear panties."

The priests had heard all this from him before. He had the longshoremen under his thumb and they had a significant vote if they could be gotten out. The priests listened because the man was quirky and you didn't want him against you. Though you didn't want him for you either.

"So home base, padres, home base," the man went on. "But stay outa beds." He began to rock a bit on his heels and his face began to flush, so they knew the story was coming. "Priest took my wife. But I found him. Waved a knife under his nose and he knew under what else. So she came back. She knew what I meant. He's a good guy now, out in the bayous, if he makes it with anybody it's in a pirogue out in the swamp where nobody sees." The flush relaxed off his face into a satisfaction. "Need guys like me," he said, looking at the two now, and not at his own story. "You take consequences with guys like me. Like I guarantee the floor everybody walks on. You walk on." He chuga-lugged the rest of his beer. "That padre on Guadalcanal, he broke, you know, right towards the end, I saw him being taken away in a jeep. Nothin' on his face but a blank. I heard later he couldn't hack it at home either. So he stepped in front of a truck. Made someone else do it for him. I shoulda talked to him, told him killers are special types, they are like pesticides, they clean things out so padres can grow flowers and the birds and the bees can do their stuff. So you just live with what you are."

He rocked a bit from leg to leg. "So I support this patsy," he said waving his hand toward the mayoral candidate across the hall. "Because the other guy's worse, the other guy's funny, he'd run from a feather, afraid it would cut him. My daughter's for the other guy, that tells you, she calls me an animal and him an angel, but I've seen angels run from a back-fire never mind a bullet, and she thinks being nice to people will do it, we'll all be in the Promised Land, so whenever we find a stiff in an alley I call her and tell her to come look. 'You do it?' she asks. 'Sounds like you.' So I say honey, you got smooth skin because of me, anybody touches you, and they all know it, and I clean 'em out and cook 'em like turkey. She spits and hangs up and goes to work for the funny guy. But she knows.

And you guys know. If I'm not around, nobody's around. Cops know it too." The flush was back on his face and his legs were spread again to give his groin room. His beer was empty. "Gotta fill this," he said, "But I tell you something else, if you guys ever ordain women like the Episcopals, you should ordain her. She knows how to keep home base. She shacked up with this guy for a while, she put him through music school, but I saw he was a creep so I sent him home to his momma. Now she's all do good. Got lines on her face to prove it and gray hair and she's never gonna have any kids, it's almost too late, so I'm never gonna see my name on anyone, an' that's too bad, some kid I could teach what holds things up. So see you guys."

He left the priests standing there with their cups of beer practically untouched. One of them turned his so the beer spilled in a stream on the floor, like an animal urinating. "Phantom," he said, "Phantom strikes again."

Choosing Baby Doe

*Wisdom has built herself a house, she has
erected her seven pillars. She has des-
patched her maidservants and proclaimed from
the city's heights: 'Who is ignorant? Let him
step this way.'*
—Proverbs 9:1, 3-4

A woman was in a futuristic business. Child design. Not design for
children, but design of children, from gene structures, before fertilization.
And not for money. She had a vision of the repair of humankind. Nature
had failed, culture had failed, it was time to try manipulation, but now
using science instead of crazy mythologies of mating. So she was aiming
for pacific types who would yet have the drive to create life, not just sit
there with the silly grin of happiness on their faces.

So far her work was computer work. Something she could do by herself. But she would soon need colleagues, people who knew the connec-
tion between types of human being and types of behavior. People who
would take her seriously. She saw a lecture advertised on campus one day,
on a kiosk outside the student union where she often went from the lab to
get her lunch. Over lunch she would watch, in a relaxed way, how the
young behaved toward one another. The lecture was in philosophy, someone speaking on beauty and truth as a Greek ideal. The man's photo was
on the advertisement, distinguished European with beard, a picture taken
some years ago most likely.

She was having yogurt and all bran plus an apple then some mint tea.
The distinguished European happened to be seated across the dining hall
with some faculty and students. Yes, his photo came from a long time ago.
He was quite withered looking, bent some, had a cane he leaned on even

from his chair, but he seemed to be extremely peaceful and quite animated. More remarkable, he seemed to be able to listen, he kept evoking student and faculty remarks as if he was eager to learn. So she wrote him a note care of the philosophy department asking him if she could see him for a short while during his stay, and she named precisely what her project was and her idea of asking him to help define a culural type she could then create through the manipulation of gene structure.

She received a note back sooner than she expected, in a quick scrawl, "Yes, but you have broken my heart, and I want to talk you out of what you are doing if I can. I say this so as not to surprise you when you come. If you still wish." He gave the number of an office in the department and when he would be there. She came at the time. His door was open and he was bent over a book on the desk, but looked up quickly when he sensed her in the doorway, before she had a chance to knock. "You are the one?" he asked. "Yes, I am the one," she said. "Please sit," he said as he himself rose out of politeness. She did. He resumed his seat. And neither said anything for the longest time.

"I want the violence to stop," she said. "I want non-raping types of men, first. Then I want non-dependent types of women. So I can have cherished kinds of children in an environment of nature that is not savaged. I want species that preserve rather than destroy. There are such. I will find out what makes them so and reproduce them genetically." "You sound so much like Plato," the old philosopher said. "However little you look like him, or at least what statues say he looked like." She shook her head slowly as if to say she had read Plato and what he had in mind was different. "You do not want to wait for some final judgment to make us all right?" he asked. She shook her head again slowly. "I have always wanted to appeal to people," he said. She shook her head slowly as if to say she had gone that route and judged it didn't accomplish much.

"I find myself defending evil," he said, "and that is what is breaking my heart." "You mean choice," she said, "you are defending choice." "Yes," he said, "and I come from the Nazi period." "I want to be sure of choice," she said. "I have been afraid of heaven for that reason," he said, "no one chooses anymore when there, people are so enchanted with the beauty of God that they are ecstatic and would not leave their ecstasy for anything." "There would be no reason to leave," she said. "Yes there would," he said.

She waited. "Someone down in hell who was thirsty," he said. She looked puzzled. "You not only have the future to deal with," he said, "you have the past, and you cannot change the genes of the past." "There is nothing behind us," she said, "they are gone. They have left us distortions we must repair." "I see them all the time," he said, "they are not gone. There are spirits loose. Maybe we must exorcise them. Free them from their own crimes even, ask them to be sorry by showing them what happened to us all after them."

"Okay," she said, "tell me the type that would do that." He saw she was adapting to his mentality in a very pragmatic way, she was willing to take his physics without his metaphysics. "I don't know," he said, "they are always a surprise to me. Just as the criminal is always a surprise to me." "Would you give up that surprise for certainty?" she asked. "No," he said. But he said it as an admission of something, very quietly. But she sensed it was also a revelation of something. "So my best type would be like you?" she asked, "yearning for choice even though I programmed it out of him or her?"

"Do you see what the essence of us is?" he asked. "Do you see your torment is an old relgious one? To the old religious we are the donkey some angel rides down a good path or some devil rides down a bad one." "There is a gene for choice, then," she said, "is that what you are saying to me? And without that gene we are donkeys?" "Not quite," he said, "not quite, I think. You have the word zombie. More like zombies." "Aren't you ashamed to continue with choice?" she asked. "And after all you've been through?" She paused a second. "Been through and survived," she continued, "survived I don't know how. Did you choose to do so?" "Yes I did," he said. "Then you're guilty of complicity," she said. "Yes, I am," he said. "All I could do was keep a certain culture alive in secret. I was useless every other way. A man asked me to be a memory. So I became one. And became invisible doing it."

"You are telling me they could all have chosen otherwise?" she asked. "Yes," he said. "And you are telling me you would preserve the choice they did make?" "Yes," he said again, so softly she could almost not hear it. "I don't want to live with such horror," she said.

"I am telling you *your* future would be a horror," he said. "You would be the only one with a memory of what you had corrected. You would be able to choose to destroy what you had made. Your genes are the old ones, if I accept your argument. You would have to purify yourself first, and that you cannot do. But if you did you would not care! Everything around you, good or bad, would be good. That was the Nazi mind, and it was done without genetic engineering. You could only choose the good!" "But I would be their evil," the woman said, "and I would want to be." "Only if you could see," he said, "only if you could remember and survive." She shook her head. "Imagine to yourself," she said, "a purified baby coming into this world, its genes all cleared of violence, its choices all selected toward the good, imagine that the baby gets known, think what a hope that would be, think what different futures than Nazi ones we could plan on." "We have already tried that," he said. "I want to try again," she said. "This time without angels and shepherds."

He looked at her and she knew he was going to say his final thing to her. "I would not want to be that baby. For all that I have gone through." She looked away from him, out the office window, there were some bare trees, some winter berries on them, some birds feeding. "I wouldn't either," she said, "now that I think." She got up and went to the door, turned and said, "I'll go back to diseases." Then she left.

21st Sunday, Ordinary Time

Cross Purposes

Wives should regard their husbands
as they regard the Lord . . .
—Ephesians 5:22

A woman was snorkeling in a cove. A crescent beach behind her, rocks to her left and right, a flat bottom twelve feet below, and ahead a bottleneck opening and the whole ocean all the way to Cornwall. "If he goes, he goes alone," she said to herself face down and her flippers moving slowly like the fins of a goldfish asleep. She saw motion below her, a lobster. She had an inner tube with a basket in it looped to her wrist by a rope. She slipped the rope, jacknifed and pumped downward, took the lobster by the midriff then let herself drift up slowly to the surface with it wriggling either end in her hand. She loved to break the surface very softly, like just appearing. She dropped the lobster in the basket, it was an okay size.

She had two others already, they must be biting one another. She tilted the basket and saw they were. "Me and him," she thought. "Okay, take your parish and go over, all of you, run from the woman clothed with the sun and the moon her footstool. Catholics like women in their places." She plunked along a bit. The water was marvelously, fiercely cold, even through the rubber suit. She loved it that way. Her husband would have nothing to do with the ordination of women. Now he had a woman bishop. O God! And he was scuttling like a lobster to get away. And he just presumed she'd follow. Until yesterday. He never even thought she thought. Well, she never thought he'd make the jump. Grousing was one thing. You can live with talk.

But yesterday was bitter. If she raised her head a little higher out of the water she could see the fish weathervane on the church, back beyond the crescent beach and fresh water pond. "I'll be damned if I'll go," she had

166

blurted. "I'll get myself ordained. And keep this church and keep those people. Not the squares. They can go with you." He was furious. And surprised into speechlessness. Adamant. No woman could ever do eucharist. Not without destroying Christianity. But he thought she agreed. "You will not ruin me," he said. "You will not stop me. There is such a thing as truth. There is such a thing as *having* to do it." "Go do it," she had shouted. "Alone!"

Neither could handle the explosion. It had never happened before. Some irritation on his part that she loved snorkeling by herself out in Atlantic water. She saw another scuttle on the bottom, she flipped again, went down, but it was too small a one so she left it. A rock cod went by, a little startled. She drifted back up to the surface. Broke it gently. There was a Catholic place to her right, a retreat house, and there were people out walking by themselves. "I will not serve," she thought. "Thus Satan to his nearest mate. O what stuff just to get through school, read John Milton who was served by women slaves! And old Jerome with his women scribes! Keep it! Keep it!" She was almost talking to the Catholics, the Anglicans too, "Keep it! Keep it!" A coke bottle tapped against her face mask. She had been thinking so intensely she didn't see. There was a cork in it and probably a kid's message headed for that coast of Cornwall. She put it in with the lobsters and lowered her face again into the water.

She was near the mouth of the cove. The floating was giving her some peace. She saw a shark skeleton. The cove floor had been sloping deeper. So this was a glimmer of a cage some thirty feet below. She flipped and headed down to see. It was not shark bone, it was human, it was held by bottom mud and by concrete boots. "Oh," she said, and blew her breath so she had to surface quickly. She sucked in some air, then dived again and came right down to the bones. But again a revulsion came over her and she said, "Oh!" and her breath went. She recognised the wide pelvis of a female skeleton. In school she and her pals had substituted a chart of one for the map of the Holy Land so when the priest said, "Now let's look at the land of Jesus," and had pulled on the cord, down came this glorious grinning female in her bones. They had roared and had had to apologize in sackcloth and ashes. Were nearly sent home. Who puts concrete boots on a female?

The woman was on the surface breathing hard. "God," she said, looking around to fix her position. This rock, that rock, then back, toward the beach, using the weather vane. "O God." She fixed her position again. "I'll never find it back. Oh who?" She flipped again, went down, took a little time but found the skeleton, reached and grabbed the skull to see if it was loose, it was, so she brought it back to the surface and dropped it over the lip of the basket afraid to look. "They might know from the teeth if I can't get back here and show them."

"Teeth," she thought. She tilted the basket. "Yes, teeth, and empty eyes. Oh!" Then, "What good is this?" She halted in the water. "Big flap, and somebody's sorrow awake again, only this time horror, murder. But I want to know who she is!" It was like a craving that welled up in her. "Put it back, honey," she heard herself say. "She's better as a mystery. You're the only one who needs to know."

"Damned if I will," she sputtered. She put her mouthpiece back in, took one more breath, dived down, located the rest of the skeleton. Again the revulsion, anger too, so she surfaced. Then in strong rhythmic kicks against the just turned tide she headed for the beach. There were some people on it. She dragged the basket on her wrist. At shallow depth she removed her flippers and put them in the basket along with her mask and snorkel, then walked up the beach quickly to her car which was up on the bank between the cove and fresh water pond. She stayed in her suit. Got the keys out from under the floor mat, climbed in and headed for the police.

She walked in the front door of the station, up to the sargeant at the desk who knew her. He broke into a smile. She often gave away lobsters. She placed the basket on his desk. It startled him a bit that she would, it was briny and weedy, dripping. So he stood. And she removed the goggles, then the flippers from the basket and stood there. He saw the lobsters. Then he saw the skull. A lobster had a claw in the eye socket. And the tail of another covered the teeth so it looked gagged. "I can show you where the rest is," she said, barely able to say it. "Oh Mrs.!" he said, and he walked around to her. "If you'll just come," she said, "I'll spot it for you." He said nothing. "Meantime give the lobsters to the poor, will you?" "I'll get you home," he said. "Find out who she is," she said. He shook his head. "She?" he asked. "I could have brought the pelvis so you'd know," she said and she started to shake. "I'm freezing." "I'll drive you," he said. "No, take care of her," she said, "and give the lobsters." She left the station and drove.

Male and Female Parts

Nothing that goes into a man from outside can
make him unclean; it is the things that come
out of a man that make him unclean.
—Mark 7:15-16

She was a commercial artist. She specialized in mannekins, head to foot. Some displays wanted only a head, some only a foot. But most wanted heads plus good hunks of torso. She had used her son as a model for several years until he finished college. He was really beautiful, she paid him well, and he paid school. He was in jail now. For statutory rape. Said he didn't know the girl was underage. But the girl's parents did when they walked in the house early and found the two. There was some violence, but her son was strong as well as beautiful, so the girl's father had a bruised face and a dislocated shoulder.

The woman sat facing a male head, a rugged, athletic looking piece, it would take a headband and goggles, a turtle neck, and a polarguard ski jacket. And it would be looking up a mountain. Perhaps some skis would go over the shoulder. So the cords of the neck had to show, and the muscles of the jaw, and there had to be an unflinching look about the eyes and a sense of hair scrambled by the wind.

She wanted to spit in its face. She moved down her bench to the woman's bust that was to go with the male. Same strength, rugged in its own way, lips parted as if getting her breath back, so her chest would be heaving some. Headband too, and goggles, t-neck, pure silk, blue with snowflake patterns, so the description read, hair to look like the Egyptian princess Nofrit, straight bangs inside the headband. She wanted to spit in its face too. Her son had been selling his beauty for a long time she now knew. She couldn't bear to meet her women friends any more. Her son's

170

customers. As for his father, he loved war, and was out somewhere in one, adviser, but he demonstrated killing by killing. When her son had phoned for bail money she had said no. She had never heard such cursing in her life and she had been an army brat and knew cursing. "No," she had said, "bail yourself out." Her mouth was dry, so, much as she wanted to spit at her mannekins she couldn't.

Then something dawned on her, cut through the turmoil in her mind. She moved back to the male bust. It would do for the sporting goods outfit who commissioned it. "It's too innocent looking," she thought, "that's why I never make it big in this business. I just do clean animals." So she picked up her spatula and began to rework the mold. She had to get a sense of corruption inside the face, but a corruption that was not obtrusive, nor an affront to health. It had to go in the eyes, the slight flare of the nostrils, the fix of the jaws, but animal-like, the look of the mountain goat or the high meadows elk. Then she moved down to the female bust. She had to make it look as if it wasn't looking, the unconcerned heat of the doe in a herd which had an impatient male. She had to look like a ruminant without a moral question. Now the woman didn't want to spit at her mannekins. She wanted to pick them up one by one and hurl them through the north window, bring down all its glass.

"They need bodies first," she said to herself. She went into the storeroom and dragged out two bodies, ones that went together like puzzles so a store could use the pieces. She took off the inoffensive, star-gazing heads and put the new heads on. But the corruption seemed to stop at the neckline. So, she got plaster and began to lay it on both until she had two sexless animals with stiffening muscles in front of her. She had to put sex on the two. "Ah, ah," she thought, and she ran to her attic where her husband had left his souvenirs. Two defused hand grenades and a dullened bayonet. But what do you do for a woman? Cymbals. Her son's cymbals from the high school band. Just cut a section in the female up to the navel and put the cymbals in and part them with the mallet he hit them with. So she worked on the statues until their sexes were as blunt as explosions or crashes. Then the girl mannekin's breast were too bland. Bell buttons. Old bell buttons. You could make her buzz, show the wires connected to the cymbals, coils, and going in the corners of her mouth as if she were a horse with a bit. Where were those old buzzers? In his toolbox under the workbench. She dragged it out. It was jammed full. So she took out a pliers, a hammer. And she turned towards her mannekins and shouted, "Speak! Speak!" and threw the tools one after the other. Then she took out a tape measure, a carpenter's level. She hurled those too, and took some chunks out of her sculpture. There was another hammer and three old fashioned buzzers below it, with a coil of wire. She got up with these in her hands and went to the mannekins still muttering, "Speak! Speak!" She was almost out of breath. "No, you have to be classical," she said, so she hit the male with the hammer on the nose and took the nose off. Then she wrenched the arms out of the female, pulled the hands out of their sockets, put the hands on top of the head as if they were fixing the hair after a bath. She was in a frenzy.

And the phone was ringing. It kept ringing as if someone knew she was there. She could almost not see it, or anything else, her eyes were flooding and her breath was short. So she just fumbled and picked it up and said nothing, though she didn't have to. It was her son and he was talking like a cascade, of gravel maybe, like off the back of a truck, or cement off the back of a truck, or smelly loam, a dump truck, that's what he was, and she was getting it. But he was saying you made me this, come and get yourself out of jail, you're a prostitute too, people make you for mannekins, you sell soul, it was like a demonic litany all written out beforehand, sure to succeed. "Okay, okay," she said, "I'll bring my money down and let us both out." She hung up. Bail was ten thousand dollars. She wrote a check for five thousand. Then she took a grenade off the male mannekin, unscrewed the top, put the check in, then restored the grenade to the male. Next she took the mallet inside the two cymbals and wrapped a second check around the handle and stuck the mallet back where it was like a tongue in a mouth. She went out and got her delivery van, put the mannekins inside, drove down to the police station and carried the two mannekins inside and said to the man behind the desk, "This is bail for my son. He'll know where to find the checks. Just call him out." She went back from the desk and leaned against the wall.

Her son was brought out. There was a crowd by this time. He looked at his mother then at the mannekins. He went to the male, took a grenade, opened it, wrong one, dropped it, took the other, opened it, right one, dropped it. Saw the amount on the check. Then went to the female, looked at the hands on the head, didn't touch them, looked down at the huge cleavage in the groin with his high school cymbals stuck in, reached down and pulled the mallet out, unwrapped the second check, then dropped both on the officer's desk. The officer examined them, picked up the phone and verified them with the bank, then with a motion of his hand gave the son freedom to go. "But not too far, kid," he added.

The son picked up the two grenades and hung them back in place. Then he put the mallet back between the cymbals in the female. "Best you could do?" he said over his shoulder. "No," she said, "you are." He picked up the male and threw it at her. The plaster, grenades, bayonet broke against the wall. Then he picked up the female and threw that so it too smashed against the wall. On the floor beside her was a jumble of male and female parts. He walked by her out the door. "You can go too, lady," the cop said softly, "after you clean this up." She came to, looked at him for a long minute, then said equally softly, "You haven't got a garbage bag, have you?"

All Eyes and Blind

Then the eyes of the blind shall be opened,
the ears of the deaf unsealed,
then the lame shall leap like a deer,
and the tongues of the dumb sing for joy.
—Isaiah 35:5-6

"He could make me see things," a woman was saying, "things that weren't there. And I knew they weren't. But they somehow were." She stopped for a second to shift in her chair for more ease. "Then after he came back from combat, the twelve months he had to serve, he turned into a block of wood, like a totem pole that was all eyes and blind." It was the therapist who shifted in his chair for more ease.

"So I took it," the woman went on, "and I can keep taking as long as I think it's not his fault, that he's been harmed. But I think it *is* his fault. And I just can't go on."

"Why do you think it's his fault?" the therapist asked.

"Oh, I couldn't answer that," the woman said, "there's a whole feeling that says so, not a whole lot of words." "Like what?" the therapist asked. "Like he's trying to make me deaf, dumb and blind. I'm like what he was, the things he saw and taught me to see, so I haunt him I guess, he just looks away from me. It's been easier recently. I don't put any flowers around anymore, and I turn out the lights when we make love. I used to love to see him and have him see me, I used to dance for him first, though we had such a small place once, I had very little room, so I was like a mime and he had to sit still on the edge of the bed. But it's dark now. It's like a feeding, like I'm a bowl of oat bran to kill cholesterol with. And we have a big place. And no babies for it. He has the Agent Orange fear and doesn't want to propagate a monster."

174

"It doesn't sound like fault," the therapist said, "sounds more like trauma."

"Okay," the woman said. "I just know I didn't do this to him. I'll carry it if he asks me. But it's like he has gone into the garden of Eden and is quietly making a desert out of it. I say quietly because you don't hear a sound when a tree falls and he's there with this buzz saw that makes no noise. Like a dance, isn't it funny? He's taken my dance to the trees and they come down like dancers sinking slowly to the earth. And he goes up to a stream with a shovel and digs a hole in the bottom sand and the water drains away. Then he scrapes the sand with no noise and the sand goes down the hole as well. Then the flowers. He has a cloth he waives that catches the scents of things, then he bundles the cloth and drops it down too. And he has something, like cords for a venetian blind. He darkens the sky a bit at a time, then jiggles it back and forth like northern lights as if he's dealing with a live audience, I mean the light is living and knows it's being shut down. Sounds weird, doesn't it?"

"Yes," the therapist said. "Tell me why you think it's fault and not trauma. I know you say it doesn't come into words, but . . ."

"Because he's merciless," she said, "and those things plead with him. You know, I think he mowed down some innocent people? Maybe people that pleaded with him? You know, I think he was told to do so? Out there? And he saw what he did? But now he's doing it and no one is telling him to? So he thinks he didn't need orders to shoot out there? That he wanted to anyway? And he thinks all the beauty he saw until that time was a cover? A cover for what he really was? And he made me into a cover? Like I was dumb as he used to be? And he wants to wake me up?"

"So you still believe in Eden?" the therapist said

The woman became aware of the therapist now, she had been so absorbed in talking about her man and the need to leave him. She looked across at him in the chair opposite. She let herself calm a bit, but did not take her eyes off him. "It's why I'm here," she said, "not there with him falling gracefully to the ground like a tree, or disappearing like things into the earth."

"We call it illusion," the therapist said, then caught himself, it was irritation that had provoked him.

"Perhaps I shouldn't be speaking to a man," the woman said, her eyes were very clear and resting very peacefully on the therapist. "You may have killed also in some war," she went on, "or voted for one, and now that's your place. It's a nightmare, if it is, and as much of an illusion as my place."

"I have not killed," he said. "I agreed with some wars."

"So, what would you restore me to?" the woman asked. "And if you say reality you'll be worthless to me or to anyone else."

"You won't let me speak," he said.

"I will," she said, "if you have some ideal, but if you don't, you won't understand except yourself."

"Ideal like what?" he asked.

"Like love," she said, "love when it's right. Not when it's cushy. I can take him in any state he's in. Except when he loves to hate. That's too insincere, don't you see? You hold what's loveable so you can hate it, or chop it down, don't you see? I don't want love on plush grass with no mosquitoes, just strawberries overhead. I'm not in it for the pleasure!"

"So you abandon him?" the therapist said. Again he caught himself, the question had come from the same irritation.

"No," she said, "have some sense." She straightened in her chair. As if she knew something had broken down in the session. "It's the other way around. I abandon him the day I give up what he used to see. There is no way back to a place that doesn't exist anymore. If I don't exist anymore for him, he is abandoned. I'm just moving out of reach. Because I can be destroyed. But only by him. He knows it. He can't destroy anything else. Nothing else loves him the way he is. And I love about him what he hates. You know, I think that's why Eden is out of reach. So we can't destroy it."

"This is a bit holier-than-thou," the therapist said, now knowing he had lost the session. He was trying to recover some pride.

"Eden isn't holy," the woman said, now on the edge of her chair. "It's shy. Like an animal that knows who kills it. Or an animal who knows who feeds it." She thought for a minute. "It's animal, and has no end." She paused again. "It's being licked by a dog. Or it's feeding a horse a carrot. Or it's cats howling in love. It's here. But it knows who kills it."

"Me?" asked the therapist.

"No," she said, rising. "He knows. You don't."

"Same thing," the therapist said.

"No," she said, "I was talking about love."

24th Sunday, Ordinary Time

One Jump Ahead of the Law

*Anyone who wants to save his or her
life will lose it; but anyone who
loses his or her life . . . for the
sake of the gospel, will save it.*
—Mark 8:35

A man found a parking ticket on his car when he came back to it. He had been at a computer session on the campus of a university. So he took the ticket and looked around and saw that the car behind his was a new arrival and clean. So he put the ticket under the windshield wiper of the other car. Chances were that the driver wouldn't look at it closely, and would either pay it or pass it on. Somebody would get suckered. As he drove away he saw the main drag was at a standstill with rush hour traffic. So he backed down his one way street to the street that led to the entrance of the university, then approached the guard with the story he was a lawyer who had to deliver an important letter to the Comptroller's office. Once on campus he cut through to easier streets on the other side.

As he was turning into traffic there he tapped another car lightly with his bumper, a scrape on the side. The other car kept moving a few yards then pulled over to examine the damage and exchange numbers. So the man did a U turn in front of a huge truck going the other way, a truck that would block any look at his licence and any view of him hanging a right down a side street. No sense stopping for minimal damage. He kept an eye on the rear view mirror to see if the red Buick he had tapped was following him. That way he didn't notice a basketball come out in the street, but did notice it when he heard the bang under his car. He slowed just a sec to see what, saw the busted basketball and some kids looking for rocks to throw and make him pay. So he sped up, did a weave, dodged the rocks, but scared an old woman driving down the other side of the street into running her car up on the sidewalk and into some neatly clipped hedges. "Take a left and go," he said to himself. So he did, but there was a huge moving van in the middle of the street, doors open and furniture out, for a fraternity house. No way to go but up on the sidewalk and cross part of a lawn. So he did as a guy with an armchair on his head gawked at him then started shouting curses. But there was the dented red Buick crossing at the next street and spotting him. He could hear the screech of tires. So the man did a U turn again, again up on the sidewalk and grass to get around the van. This time the one with the armchair on his head tried to throw it but missed, then used some new curse words until a horn blast from behind scared him silly, the dented Buick trying to get over the same lawn. Meantime the first guy took a right down the basketball street. And there were the kids with the busted balloon. They spotted him instantly and heaved the broken thing at him, in the window but it just glanced off the headrest. He got to the street alongside the campus, drove to the gate, gave the same hurry story about a letter to the Comptroller, then whizzed through campus to the original gate where the cop recognised him and waved to say I knew I could trust you.

He spotted the red Buick behind a ways. So he drove to his original one way street, went down it, saw his former parking spot was open, whipped into it, cut the engine, went back to the car behind, took the ticket and put it again on his own car, then headed on foot between two houses where he could hide and watch what happened. Sure enough, the red Buick came up and stopped like a dog at a hydrant and a man got out to look at the car. He felt the hood. It was hot. But so was the weather. He took the ticket out from under the windshield wiper and checked the date and time and violation, then went to look at the plate numbers. They matched. Then he replaced the ticket and returned to his own car and drove off still like a suspicious dog. So the man in hiding knew he couldn't move for a while. Just then the traffic police came by again and put a second ticket on his car. Then in a few minutes the red Buick came cruising by, still like a suspicious dog.

The man couldn't stay between the houses or other kinds of police would come. So he walked nonchalantly over to the university cafeteria, had some coffee, then walked back in time to see a third ticket being written. The guy in the red Buick was talking to one of the cops and pointing to matching dents on bumper and side door, but the police were pointing to the three tickets and shrugging their shoulders. As soon as they moved on, the man went quickly to his car, unlocked the door, unlocked the hood, reached in, pulled a few wires, closed the hood, locked the door, escaped between the houses, then phoned in to a Triple A garage to come tow the car, phoned the police to explain why he hadn't moved it, said he had been too busy to call in right away. Next, he took a cab home, made himself a drink, sat in a chair to watch the evening news and lived happily ever after.

Live Bait

*If the virtuous man is God's son, God
will take his part and rescue him from
the clutches of his enemies.*
—Wisdom 2:18

A man was fishing. There were some trout in the pond. Somewhere. He rarely did this. His father had, a lot, and the man had his father's equipment, old and comfortable, even the hat with the plugs and sweat grooved in so the leather was two-toned. This was peace, his father had said. The slow whip of the rod, the light buzz of the reel, silver light on nylon, and the plop of the fly out where some circles of water had been made by a fin or an insect just gobbled. Then the little bit of trawling, the lure winking at some fish, then the process all over again. Until a fish. Then the taut line, the unyielding wind of the reel, a trout thrashing, dancing in the air right up to his hand, the unhooking of the mouth, the throwing back in.

He always threw the fish back in. His father had not, he loved trout meat, he had a special pan to poach them in, or fry them in oil, or he had wrap so he could bake them under the charcoal he brought. He was superb then at filleting them so not a tasty morsel was missed. But the son was not like the father. He could catch but not kill. Though he ate what he didn't see killed. And goose eggs. His father loved them. And cabbage with turnip and parsnips plus the hunk of ham and potatoes. It was a noisy meal with the hot food on the tongue needing air to cool it, so his father drew in air as a dog does water. Then looked roguishly guilty at the slurp. Life had been a delicious meal for him, even the harshness of it was buttermilk or a raw egg floating in a glass of port wine. And death had been sacred, like the death of a trout, his would feed someone somewhere, he

181

had said, one of the souls in Purgatory, or someone in despair on earth. It might even be a comfort to the Crucified One who knew two thousand years ago that some companionship would come from another dying man. The man fishing spotted a small flick on the surface out about twenty yards, so he reeled in a few feet of line, then in the classic motion he had been taught he cast so he landed gently right on the nose of the ripple and it wasn't two seconds before a strike. He drew a furrow across the water towards himself, then lifted the wriggling fish out of the water and got ready to realease it. But he didn't. He put it instead in the basket beside him. He was hungry. He had plenty of other food. But life was eating him. And he wanted some small revenge. Not the white meat of a trout. He fished some more and got three for a total. He took his Coleman stove and balanced a pan of water on it and he poached the three fish until the flesh was soft and loose. Then with his knife he teased the pieces free and ate them like an Indian scout, squatting on his heels, leaning against a rock. Cleaning the fish had been no problem, cooking them less, but eating them was a grief, not a pleasure. Yet they took care of the hunger. The bones go for whoever wants them. "So, cancer, how do you like them fish?" he said as he rattled things clean at the water's edge. He could already feel the rumbling in his stomach. "They're eating me." In two days time a section of that stomach would come out. "So I'm the fish then," the man said. There were lots of ripples now on the water. The sky had darkened, the fish could see better, the insects were impervious to the danger. "But not for someone's food." He put his head down on his knees, he was back squatting against the rock. He could feel tears. "I'd rather be someone's food." Then he looked up. "But I guess I was," he thought. "That man ate his way through me too. He lived without thinking. And I thought without living." He sat still for a long time. "I have to make it up," he thought.

He rose from his position and walked to the water's edge. He took the knife he had used to clean and eat the fish. He pricked his thumb lightly with it so a bead of blood formed, then he placed his hand flat on the water which was wonderfully clear. He saw the small cloud the blood made in the water. It was like fish sperm only dark and had just sand to fertilize. The cold of the water quickly closed the wound. He opened the wound lightly two more times, for each of the fish. A small, small cloud of blood on the water. Then with his forefinger he wrote his name, the water making the gentle slurp his father had made eating the boiled dinner. And there were trout there, a few feet away, edging in towards his fingers. The light was so that they could not see him, or he looked like a rock, but they could see the motion of his fingers, the traces they made on the water. He saw the marvelous delicacy of their tails, their dorsal fins, and the way they floated in the shallow water they had. So he kept his hand moving gently like some unaware insect, a water spider or dragonfly. A trout made a swift lunge, nipped his finger, realized its mistake and shot back out into deep water. The other trout scattered too. "So no regrets," the man said as he stood to relax his taut hamstrings. "And no revenge." He looked at the ball of his thumb and saw the red nick now closed plus some scraping from the fish bite on his forefinger. "Trout bites man," he thought, "good headline."

He took off his father's fishing jacket, took off the fishing hat, then stripped off his own clothes and waded into the cold water. His stomach was now paining him. He began to swim, breast stroke—into the water, out of it, into the water, he was at eye-level with insects, at eye-level with trout. The water was nipping at him, the air as well. "I could stop right here," he thought, "feed the pond. But someone would drag me out and wrap me in concrete." He turned back toward shore. He coughed up a bit of food. "Not bad," he thought, "some stayed. It's a hope."

He crept in the water right up to the shore like a mammal looking to live on land. Then he stood up and walked to his clothes. He felt a great hunger for his father's presence. But he did not put on the fishing jacket nor the hat, just his own clothes. He turned back toward the water. "I have been afraid to eat," he said to it. "But you haven't." He waited. "You think you can keep me down?" He waited some more. "You're going to have to. You or your friend the ground. Or your friend the air." There was a flurry of ripples out some yards. "I'd throw you back now," he said. "Bet you never thought of it. Catch you and throw you back." There were some more ripples. "Be glad I'm not my father," he said, and turned and left.

26th Sunday, Ordinary Time

The Shock of Choice

It was a burning fire that you stored up
as your treasure for the last days.
—James 5:3

A woman was a money buff. Paper money especially. Though she had gotten into ancient coins too, they had fascinating histories, and could often be picked up on the sly in the old world and smuggled home. She did not have the wealth for museum pieces so she wasn't cheating humanity of cultural links. She was a bank executive. Her specialty was in bank transfers. She had to watch money so it would stay clean. That is why she had to know the actual paper, not just entries on a computer screen. And she had to watch money so it would stay real, not be counter-feit.

Counterfeit was what she saw one day, brilliant, brilliant counterfeit. She said so to the CIA man sitting across the desk from her. The serial numbers were slightly illogical. Dollars had many patterns, but not quite these. The printing would never give the forgery away. In fact she would swear these were printed by the US Government itself. Except for the numbers glitch. The denomination of the bills was large, blocks of hundreds. The man thanked her, closed his attache' case, said the matter would now be turned over to the FBI. He got up to leave. "What kind of fool do you think I am?" she said to him. And she waited. He had stopped at the door before opening it. "You printed that money, and you're going to do something dirty with it," she continued. "It's going to come back through this bank and I'm going to spot it and phone the FBI who are going to tell me to let it go through and then tell them where it goes. Like putting something radioactive in the blood stream. Then following it to the heart." "Yes," the man said. "We also knew you would figure it out and do

184

the right thing." "That's blood money," the woman said, "drugs or assassination or arms. Nothing doing! I tell the press."

The man walked very calmly back to the chair before her desk and sat down. "We're buying drugs so we can get higher and higher up the chain of production," he said, "then we're selling them to get higher and higher up the chain of distribution. We pay in fake money that will fool everyone but you or someone like you. A rare few. And we sell for real money. As we increase the operation we will flood the drug king world with counterfeit. Then one day let it out and cost them their power." "But the drugs get used, don't they?" she said. "We have to pay a price," he answered, "this is not a free game." "You don't pay a price," she said, "an addict does."

The man was silent, a silence that said something. She read it, "They may as well be of some use whether they know it or not, right?" she said. "Right," he answered, "they are gone anyway. We might as well get some use out of them." "You know what I think?" she said, "I think you don't want to catch anybody. You'd be bitterly disappointed if this game were over. It's *your* drug, this game!" "You think what you want," he said, "you do what we say. Or you do nothing anymore. You understand?" "Yes," she said. "And I understand how to take you out with me. Not just you personally." "We have all the exits covered," he said. "I mean that figuratively. We know what can happen to you and your family. And if you think you're recording this conversation, I have a jammer in this case. So you let these bills through when they come. Think of it as doing good, whatever you think our motives are."

She was smiling at the man. It caused the first break in his composure. He looked at her without another word for a while. "So you work for them too," he said. She kept smiling, maybe even a little more. "So you can tell us who," he said. Still nothing from her. "And you can tell them." Nothing from her. "Why don't I just take you in," he went on. "We can just work you free of what you know and have you back here without a scratch." He was speaking with absolute confidence again. Still nothing from her but a secure smile. "They must keep an eye on you," he said, now with doubt again.

"Let me tell you," she said, "save you an hour guessing. I never tell them where I put their money. They pay to have it cleaned. You touch me and billions disappear. You touch me and you disappear. So you take that fake money and burn it. And you tell me the numbers of the real money. I'll clean it for you too. But the percentage is high." He was staring at her. "Robin Hood," he said, "you're Robin Hood." "And you're Mickey Mouse," she said, "and they're Captain Kangaroos. And this whole filthy thing is going to float some flowers or else." There was a pause. "Or else what?" he said. "Cremation," she said, and she pointed to the attache' case of bills in his lap. His face lit with triumph. "You know you are already damned," he said, "you burn either way." "But you don't," she said. The shock of the choice immobilized him. "Jesus!" he said, "you do this for a living?" He was staring at her. "You God?" "Depends," she said. "Depends on what?" he asked. "What you do with that money," she answered.

Getting Rid of Girl Things

*. . . anyone who does not welcome the
kingdom of God like a little child will
never enter it.*
—Mark 10:15

"I want some sugar," a boy said. He had oatmeal in front of him, cream
on it, a spoon in it already. "Use the honey," his mother said as she turned
her typewritten pages at the other end of the table. "I hate honey," the boy
said, softly, like someone aware of human flashpoints. His mother looked
up. "Use the honey," she said, "it's better than sugar. But you should eat
cereal as it is. Best for you." "Is not," he said, again softly. "Then don't
eat," she said. He started to slide off the chair. "Eat," she said. "Use the
honey." She turned a page. A new novel. Her writing put food on the
table. So don't distract her while she was keeping them alive.

The steam was gone from the oatmeal and the cream was separating out
into milk and water, it looked like. "It's cold," he said. She got up, came
over, took the spoon out of the bowl, went to the electronic oven, put the
bowl inside, nuked it, then brought it back steaming. She took the honey
stick and dripped honey right in the middle of the mound of oatmeal where
it rose above the milk. "Eat around it if you don't like it," she said and
went back to her absorption in her text. "Have to go to the toilet," he said.
She looked at him. Then looked down at her pages. He held himself. She
had made him clean up the last time. "Have to go," he said. "Okay," she
said, "then right back here, and you eat whether it's cold or not."

He slid off the chair, went to the bathroom, closed the door, got himself
ready, then up on the seat. He wasn't tall enough to stand. Outdoors he
was. He could play firehose outdoors. Indoors he could only play girl. He
didn't aim straight. So some shot out and onto the floor. He climbed

187

down, got some paper, cleaned up, then flushed everything down. He noticed how alone he was. How she made no noise outside. She was reading her text. There were just girl things in the bathroom, hanging to dry. Though a dryer looked like a gun. Boy things had gone. She had thrown them right out the window. He was in the doorway that day and she had nearly thrown him. She was screaming big, bad words and tearing in and out, he didn't know where to stand, she just shoved him out of the way and everywhere was in the way.

He climbed over the rim of the bathtub to see if he could open the window. A bad window, it was frosted and you couldn't see out and only a little light came in. But it did open to him as he stood precariously on the other rim. There was a frosted window across from his, and a well in the building dropping to the rear entrance, the garbage cans and the walkway to the garages. He took a bottle of shampoo off the tub rim and held it out the window then dropped it. It hit the tin lids of the garbage cans, a wonderful crunch. So he took some conditioner and dropped that. Another crunch then a further splat as it bounced. He hoisted himself a bit and looked over the window sill. It was like being in a bomber in the movies on TV. There was the city below. He took a hair cap off the shower rack and dropped it and watched, like a parachute gone crazy. There was a wind in the well of the building to chase the cap around. He got back in the tub and reached to pull her drying things down. A bra first. He reclimbed to the window and dropped it to hit one of the ashcans, but it didn't hit, it landed on the sidewalk and looked like a soldier shot he had seen in a picture book. He took some panties and aimed them but they missed too, they looked like another man shot on the ground but pink like he didn't have any clothes on. Then he took a slip and it fell beside the others, so now the things looked like people washed up by a flood on the News last night during supper when she had made him eat the ucky fish while she did several things at the same time.

He got down from the window again, moved a stool so he could get to the medicine cabinet. He took some bottles of pills, went back to the window, poured the pills so he could see them bouncing off the lids below, rattle, rattle, then all over the place, some of them actually running like wheels along the sidewalk. And the capsules did funny things. But the vaseline just went guck, and stuck to what it hit. So he took soap but it wasn't very interesting. Then toilet paper. He held one end of the roll and it streamered as he watched it, it hit, it kept rolling until it wore out or stuck in something. Then he let the end go and it settled like the icebergs he saw, but faster. And everything was gone from the bathroom, combs, brushes, creams—they went guck like the vaseline—and panty hose, they were really dead men down over the bushes. He loved what he saw as he hung out more from the window, it was like from an airplane during the war.

He felt a grab at his shorts, his mothers nails cutting into the small of his back as she jerked him from the window. He went down into the tub with a clunk of his head before she could grab him with her other hand. She was staring at him like some fierce African cat he had seen on her nature programs. He rolled into a ball for protection as he had seen the porcupines do, and some gas escaped from his bowels. He felt like a small skunk he had also seen. His eyes were closed in self protection. His head hurt. Nothing happened. He opened his eyes. She was still staring at him, but not fiercely now, more like that day his Daddy had gone, she was vacant again like that, but looking at him. She was making a choice, he could feel it, to throw him out the window too maybe. He'd be happier bouncing off the garbage lids like the shampoo and the pills except he knew it would hurt. It didn't hurt things, just people.

She was now very calm and not staring. Her eyes were very soft and filled with feeling, like the dog's he had seen licking its cubs on TV. He wanted one but she said, "You're lucky people let *you* live here." She knelt slowly at the edge of the tub. "You want to throw me too?" she asked. "You could get Daddy to help if I'm too heavy." He started to choke on the tears that shot onto his face. He couldn't breathe or cry. His whole being was pain and she disappeared from sight. "You're a baby," he heard her say. He shook his head no. "Stand up, then" she said. He moved slowly because he couldn't do otherwise, but he stood, his mouth still open, his face suffused, he knew he couldn't hold much longer. "You want me?" she asked. He nodded instantly. "Come," she said and reached her hand. He put his in hers, got over the rim of the tub and followed her back out to the kitchen.

"So what about some french toast?" she asked. "I have maple syrup left I didn't throw out." He knew it was his Daddy's maple syrup and his

Daddy's french toast. He nodded. There was still a silence to him, and it was filled with pain. "Take me a minute," she said. "You want to go play or sit here?" He climbed up into his chair. "I love Daddy," she said as she started to get things ready, bowl for the eggs, a beater, bread, a nice iron pan, the snap of the gas stove lighter. Then the noise and the motion of her from here to there and he following her every move with his eyes and wet face. "He loves somebody else," she said as she dipped the bread in the beaten eggs and milk. "But he loves you in spite of somebody else." The boy felt some of the pain go. "But he doesn't love me," she said, and the boy could smell the warm french toast and the warming syrup she had put in a small pot on the next burner. "You love me?" she asked. He nodded.

She took two beautiful slices out of the pan, put them on a plate she had warmed on the stove, and brought them to him with the syrup. He didn't even see them. He was looking up at her. And she knew why. But she couldn't say it. "Shall I pour?" she asked. He nodded. "Say when," she said. He was still just looking at her, not the syrup. She dropped the syrup pot onto the plate and just picked him out of the chair and held him. "I can't say it," she said. And she held him tighter. Then, "I have some of your french toast?" "Yes," he said and turned in her arms towards the plate. She put him down in the chair, got another chair, another knife and fork, and she ate one toast while he ate the other. "Mmmm," she said. He kept his eyes on her as he ate. His face was all smeared with maple syrup." "Slob," she said. And he beamed.

Beauty Is As Beauty Pleases

. . . the Spirit of Wisdom . . . Compared
with her, all gold is a pinch of sand, and
beside her silver ranks as mud.
—Wisdom 7:9-10

A man had sought wisdom all his life. And the one thing he knew toward the end was that beauty was the most precious of all the things of the earth. And it was the most treacherous. It abandoned you always for someone else. As if it were keeping itself alive from generation to generation, then dropping its used containers in the trash. He felt like trash, his body like a crumpled aluminum foil. But his senses still worked. He could still spot the fugitive, beauty, as it ran from tree to tree, or parent to child.

"You are afraid of death," he said to it one day. "Afraid to lose your lovely puss." He saw anger out there and knew he had struck. "Did I leave a mark?" he asked. "That's not what I want. Anyone can leave a mark. I'll kiss it." He kissed the wind going by him. "There," he said, "you look nice again. A little feminine. A little young. Wet nose like a deer." He moved himself on the park bench. It was hard on his bottom. "Need a cushion," he said. "Used to have buttocks, but they go when you can't eat much." He paused, then said, "No, that's not true. You don't eat much, do you? And you've a bottom as round as a baby's." He waited. "But you are a joy, you damn coward!" he said turning on the bench to see a man with an Irish setter on a leash go loping together across the grass. "No," he went on, "You're not all flesh. You're thought. So you can run faster and hide. My mind is like oatmeal. Tastes like it without milk. You used to be like brandy. Now you're like mush."

191

He got up, did a little stagger for his balance, then looked at a swaying poplar over near the tennis courts. "Don't look," he said to the tree, "you're next." Then he felt sad, looked back at the tree and said, "I wouldn't wish it. I'm sorry. Keep your eye on those tennis players. Stay young. Where was I?" He started along the path. "Yes, my coward," he said. He stopped for a chipmunk who sped into a wall then popped its head back out to look. "Exactly like me," he said, and pointed his finger at it. The wall swallowed it again. "Exactly," the man said, pointing at the wall. It had a green lichen on it now turning rust from the recent cold snap. "Exactly like me," the man said and started toward it to touch it and see how dry it was, but felt a twinge and saw the uneven footing. "Exactly," he said and pointed at his own feet. There was dog poop on one of them. "Okay puddle, here I come," he said.

He walked to the other side of the path and plunked his foot down in some watery grass. A nice squish. "I hurt you," he said. "I'm shoving it in your face. I shouldn't." He removed his foot and saw the print fill with water. "What will I do?" he asked. "You grow again? It's almost too late. Snow will have to come. Freeze my foot on you." He began to tamp around the edges of his footprint to spring the footprint loose. And he did, he raised the muddy grass in the middle. "Now you look more like it. A little shitty maybe. But that'll dry up and blow away."

He started walking slowly again. "So where are you, my little coward?" he said, scuffing his foot every now and then to clear it. "You in that woman? She opens her blouse her breasts will fly off. Like red baloons. O, she's cream!" He stopped and felt a choke. "My own she chased you, you coward, and you licked her dry like a cat and left the saucer for me. What have I got to fill it?" He swallowed. "Okay, I'm glad. I had a taste. And this one, look at her bounce. She's got a taste too. Then, you cat, you go up on a roof where no one gets you." He started again. "I'm the one on my shoe," he said. "So okay, run, run, so everyone can see you. Don't let death catch you. I'll trip him up so you can get away. Do a cross block on him. He'll hit the floor like an egg!" The man lifted his arm like a nose guard. His joints cracked. He giggled. "Hear him?" he said. "I just hit him one." He lowered his arm. "Suppose I take him with me? You stop running?" He paused for an answer. "No," he said, "because you wouldn't believe me. You still think I want revenge." There was a minute while he walked slowly toward the exit from the park. "I'll take him with me anyway. You do what you like." He was near the street. "Death's always running at you, like these cars. Look him in the eye and he swerves. Or he hits you and you take his fun away. You don't blink. You don't hold onto anything."

The man got to the crosswalk outside the park and pushed the pedestrian button. "This is for lightning bugs," he said, "make it halfway. Then a desert island until somebody else comes." There were some screeches as cars stopped for the light. "This is power," the man said as he started across, "with mortals cursing me from inside cages. Wild animals cringing at my feet. You see, beauty, what happens when you're brave?" He made it to the island just as the light switched and there was a screech of tires as the cars took off. "When you're brave, you know what hits you," he said. He drew in a deep breath of fresh carbon monoxide. "That's cynical," he said. "When you're brave, you hit nothing." The light changed for him again to cross the rest of the way. "Goodbye, beauty," he said. "Don't step on anything. You'd have to stop."

29th Sunday, Ordinary Time

"You Killed My Mommy!"

*. . . we must never let go of the faith we
have professed. For it is not as if we had
a high priest who was incapable of feeling
our weaknesses with us; but we have one who
has been tempted in every way that we are,
though he is without sin.*
—Hebrews 4:14-15

A woman was in a tea shop near the State House. An old Bullfinch design with red brick and gold dome. And there were tea shops. She was a representative and had just voted no on a death penalty bill. The bill had failed to pass. And as she left the chamber there were people screaming in rage at her. Relatives of victims. It was their rage she refused to satisfy. The guilty could be locked away. The hell with the cost. It came out of liquor taxes. The rage of the relatives staggered her. She was young, a lawyer, already had a broken marriage, a bitter taste from that, but she had a sense she wanted a life of public service. That meant having warm hands and a cold heart. She went to the tea shop because it had flowers hanging from pots and canaries in cages. Someone ran it for ritual's sake as well as for profit. She was half way through a delicious cup of Darjeeling when a girl of about eight just appeared at her shoulder and said, "You let them kill my mommy." The words were like a blow to the stomach. The woman turned slightly in her chair, put a hand on the girl's shoulder to hold her there, then looked around for the cause of this. There, outside the window, were three people, an elderly couple, and a man about the woman's own age. "You bastards!" she muttered to herself. Her hand was very gentle on the girl's shoulder. She moved the girl toward the chair across the tiny table and said, "Please sit and tell me." The girl was a little afraid and looked back out the window for some sign. The three of them came through the door and got into position around the table. "So tell me," the woman said. She was aware that the canary just over her head was silent and flipping back and forth in its cage. And the flowers seemed to want to close. "Don't have to," the younger man said. "It's all the rapes and murders and the guys that do them walking around the street with a free pass from you." The older couple were flushed with both grief and anger.

"Little girl," the lawyer said looking down, "what do you want me to do." The father started to speak but the woman cut him off. "Shut up," she said, "I want to see how far you took her. Little girl," she resumed, "what do you want me to do?" "I want you to execute them." The girl said it perfectly. "Do you know what that means?" the lawyer said. The man started to interrupt again, but the lawyer snapped, "I listen if she talks. I do not listen if you do. That's the way you set it up." She calmed herself and said again with great softness to the girl, "Do you know what execute means?" The girl was uneasy, maybe frozen a bit. "Look," the woman said, "see that canary? What would it be to execute that canary?" The three elders exploded into speech, "That's what a victim is, innocent, caught in a cage, some stinking rat reaches in and kills it! She found her mother when she came home from school!" There was a silence then as tense as a thunder storm.

The lawyer stood slightly and unhooked the cage from its hanger and lowered it to the small table. She pushed the flowers and her tea to the side. Then she opened the cage and gently put her hand into it and waited for the bird to calm. Then in slow motion closed her hand around the bird and brought it out, its head showing through the collar her hand made around its neck. It's eyes were blinking rapidly. The woman stroked the head with the forefinger of her other hand. "Now I want you to reach your hand and hold the head of the bird between your thumb and finger. Then I want you to squeeze as if to make your fingers meet. I will hold the bird and you will break its neck." The girl recoiled back on her father. "You stinking thing!" the father shouted, and everyone in the tea shop looked, "that bird is her mother. You're the goddam killer!" "This bird is safe in my hands, little girl," the lawyer said. And there were tears on her face from the man's stinging words. "I would never kill it. Nor would I ever kill anything else. Because this is our life, yours and mine." She opened her hands and the canary flew up toward the ceiling, then across the ceiling to the drapery rod over the tea shop window where it landed in fright, its eyes rolling.

"Now look," she said, "I have a man's head where the bird was. He's the one who killed your mommy. Now tell me to squeeze. And tell me what happens to me if I do." The girl was beyond her understanding and she looked up to the father for a clue. But the lawyer got to him first. "Tell me to squeeze, you son of a bitch! Use me as your goddam executioner! Then go out and see if you can wipe the blood off her mind with more blood! Then see if you can wash it off me!"

"A murderer has no right to life!" said the man, said it like a cold chisel. "You don't either," said the lawyer, "not to my life, not to hers. We are not your hot seats." She pointed to the little girl. "You used her on me. She's dead from you, not from that goddam rapist. Look at her, she's eight and she wants to execute and doesn't know what it means, but you own her, you three, and she does what you say! Well I don't!" "I hope you get it," said the man as he started his group toward the door, "maybe you'll understand!"

"If I do, I'd like you to see it!" the lawyer said, "make you feel good." She stood up and walked toward him. "In fact, *you* could do it. Out in the alley. They could watch you." She reached out and grabbed him by the lapels of his suit jacket. "Then maybe *you'd* understand!" He pulled her hands away and stood glaring at her. Then looked aside. Then back and said, "I went too far." They were blocking the doorway into the shop. He moved a bit but she didn't. "No," she said, "no! You turned into something. And that's why I vote the way I do." Now she moved a bit and she looked down at the little girl. "Your choice," she said, "gun or girl." Then walked back to her table and stood until they left. She hung the cage up again, its door open. She paid. Put on her jacket. But didn't move. She was in someone's fist. She didn't know whose.

30th Sunday, Ordinary Time

Blood Pudding, Not Apple Sauce

. . . he can sympathize with those who are
ignorant or uncertain because he too lives
in the limitations of weakness.
—Hebrews 5:2

A man was picking apples. He had a dozen trees out behind his house. He loved to care for those trees. Most of the apples he gave away. To the reformatory down the road. The town was old Yankee and the prison site almost as old, its walls red brick and its cell blocks Georgian architecture. His real work was in Boston where he was an admiralty lawyer. "I'm perfect Gilbert & Sullivan," he thought as he climbed the ladder rungs higher into one of the trees. "Never been to sea." The apples were glorious this year. As he picked a branch it was like releasing a bird from a coop. There was a hoot from the prison. Someone loose. No one ever ran from that place. Stern as it looked it was minimum security. Maybe someone from out in the fields. Prisoners did the truck gardening over a wide area. The State owned patches of ground here and there. There was not much to worry about. Escapees from this place never took hostages or harmed anyone. They were the fraud type.

"Buddy, all I want is the keys to your car," he heard a voice under him say. "And don't look or I'll pull the ladder on you." So the man in the tree kept his face toward the apples on the branch in front of him. He said, "Car's in the driveway. Under the front bumper is a key. In a magnetic case. Just to the right of the number plate. There's a suede jacket in the trunk and an Irish tweed hat. Some dark glasses on the dashboard. Put 'em on and you might even make it to Worcester. But they got you, friend." "I

197

just need two hours, buddy," said the voice below him. "A little wedding to go to. And buddy, no phone calls. People get killed at high speed." "She marrying someone else?" the man in the tree said. His question stopped the prisoner a few feet away from the tree which concealed the two men from each other. "You going to do damage?" said the man in the tree. The hooting from the prison got in between each word. "Just ruin it," the prisoner said. "You want her and you can't have her anymore, right?" said the man in the tree. He had almost to shout. "I don't want her," the prisoner shouted back. There were sirens mixing in with the hoots. And a lot of them, and the sounds of screeching tires in the distance. "The whole State's coming," said the man in the tree, "they love you." He knew the prisoner had not moved. "I'm coming down, okay?" he said. No answer. So the man in the tree lowered himself slowly, his canvas bucket across his chest half filled with macintosh.

He stood at the foot of the ladder and did not turn to look. "What do you want?" he said over his shoulder to the prisoner. It really did sound now as if the whole countryside was up, as if the Redcoats were coming and word was out to the Minutemen. "I want to shame her," the prisoner said, said it with a swiveling head, the man from the tree thought. "Then go, friend, and good luck," he said. "What's a good road west?" the prisoner asked. "Better tell me or you'll have a heap of junk." "This is not you," the man from the tree said and he turned to look at the prisoner who was all covered with blood. And looking at him as if through a mask of caked paint. And the prisoner's clothing was also streaked. "That's not paint," the man from the tree said. The prisoner stood there without moving, and he was now staring at the man from the tree daring him to figure the blood out. "It's not fresh blood either," said the man from the tree." "No," the other exploded. "You want to walk into the wedding all bloody," the man said. "Yes," the prisoner exploded again. "She kill someone?" the man asked. "Yes," the prisoner said. It came out like a shot. "You taking the rap?" the man said. "No," the prisoner said, "I stole too much." "For her?" the man said. "Yes," the prisoner said. "Who'd she kill?" the man said.

The prisoner twisted a bit. Not to check out the hoots and sirens. Twisted from something inside. "Baby?" the man said. And the prisoner's fists shot up in the air and started beating it but not in frenzy, more like someone beating a ceremonial drum with invisible mallets. "Now she wants to be clean!" the prisoner shouted. "Make-believe!" he shouted louder.

"You're going as the baby!" the man from the tree said above the noise of the manhunt. "Yes!" said the prisoner, "I'm going!" He started, but around in circles. "Where'd you get the blood?" the man from the tree said. "It's mine," the prisoner answered. "Took a little out every day." He knew he was trapped in that orchard. And his gesture was blocked. "I have a camera," said the man from the tree. "Polaroid. I'll take some shots if you give up." "I'll take some shots," the prisoner said, "run right at 'em." The man from the tree knew the prisoner would provoke a hail of bullets. "You got a gun?" he asked. "Better than a gun," the prisoner said, still walking around himself. "It's for kids," he said as he took out a plastic automatic, "kids to play with. So they can be real." It was a real looking toy. "I'll take a shot of you and keep it," the man from the tree said. "I'll show it to the judge and tell him you flipped and why."

The prisoner stopped. "You think you understand why?" he said to the man, words like compressed air. "You love her," the man said, "you loved that baby. She's wiped out one by abortion. She's wiping out the other by marriage. She's wiping you out." "You promise?" the prisoner asked. There was now grief in his voice. "I promise," said the man. "Then get the camera," said the prisoner. "Before the blood falls off. I tell you her name. I tell you her address. You send it, right?" "No," said the man. "I keep it. I show it to a judge. Then I give it to you. Then you think how much damage more you want to do." The prisoner stopped his circling movements. Near a pile of apples poured on a canvas tarp. He sat down on the edge of the tarp and fell back on the apples. "Get the goddam camera," he said, "and call 'em on the phone." "Throw me the toy," the man said, "or they'll make you apple sauce." The prisoner threw it. "Not apple sauce," he said, "blood pudding. The way she did."

31st Sunday, Ordinary Time

Last of the Innocents

The second [commandment] is this:
You must love your neighbor as yourself.
—Mark 12:31

A woman had jury duty. It was for a week if she didn't get chosen for a long trial. There were three on the agenda. Plus the standard short ones that filled the calendar of every court. She was scrutinized for the rape case. Defense dismissed her without a question, a look seemed to be enough. Same way for the espionage case the next day. Same way for the racketeering. The man indicted was a regional boss. Defense took one look at her and she was dismissed. "They know I don't want to be there," she thought. "They know my mind's somewhere else."

It was on herself in fact. She was pregnant. Surprise! She had thought she was safe. Some recreation in middle age for herself, a careerist in marketing. And her instincts were to let the pregnancy continue. Spring fashions had actually gotten boring. "Think of it as a sabbatical," she thought. "In the Costa del Sol near Malaga. Or on Majorca, in the north of the island, sugar brown earth and lemon trees, the tinkle of goat bells and paradisal weather." That's what defense in the rape case had spotted, her happiness, she'd never concentrate, or if she did, she'd resent the gory details and vote guilty out of revulsion and run for home.

The guy who was the father of her baby was married, not well, but in his business he had to stay smooth or people wouldn't trust him with their money. So why tell him more than she was going to live in Europe and get some fresh ideas. Invite him over anytime, knowing he couldn't come, a perfect cover. Then give the baby away after she saw how neatly she'd done it. "Should be perfect," she was thinking as the espionage defense waved her away. And when the racketeering defense said no she was think-

200

ing, "Majorca. Up the switchback roads over the mountains then down to Soller, the harbor, and back then to Fornalux, lovely little town in a hollow. Know just the house, just the street, no heating, but some down blankets and clothes and daytimes leaning against a sun heated wall while I grow this apple inside."

"Three down, two to go," she thought further, but still didn't click as to why she was being dismissed. Nobody can see pregnancy for a while. The fourth day she was asked to sit on a landlord/tenant case which barely got going before the landlord ceded. Some information he had not suspected was coming out and he wanted to stop more of it, so he had his lawyer concede and the judge set the damages. On the fifth day she was chosen for a case she didn't expect. It was a paternity suit. Change of venue kind of case because the people were well known politically where they came from. A mayor and a city councilor. It was going to drag. Lawyers from both sides accepted her, again just by looking and seeing a certain happiness in her. Defense thought she would therefore not be anti-male. And the plaintiff's lawyer that she would be pro-female.

But the woman was shocked out of her happiness. She asked to see the judge, not to get out of jury duty for the duration of the trial, but to tell him she had a built in bias against a woman who would not give a child away she couldn't take care of. When you go after the man like this, you want damages, money and his reputation. That's love turned hate. The prospective woman juror was having her baby to see how well her body would do, then would give the child to someone who would cherish it, and her next neat contribution to the world would be accomplished. The judge was conservative, but he loved life, not himself. The woman could tell she angered him. "A necessary evil," she thought, "but I would skew the case. He knows it."

He didn't say anything. He seemed to be back inside his head thinking. Then his eyes narrowed from infinity to her. "I'm going to leave you on the jury," he said. She felt a flash of anger of her own go through her, but she could control it she knew. She waited for him to say why. He didn't. She reached for her purse which was beside the chair and got ready to rise, but he could see her question: "Won't you get a flawed verdict?" "The judge is the ultimate decider in a case," he said quietly. "Then someone judges him. Or her."

"What judgment are you making on me?" she asked. "I guess I take a certain joy in you," he said. She relaxed in her chair a bit, an involuntary sort of move. "There is going to be a lot of love thrown around that courtroom like curses in a brawl," he said. "A baby is going to be a criminal exhibit. Intercourse is going to be the result of false advertising. Love play is going to be influence peddling. And here I'll have someone on the jury who's happy she had intercourse, who didn't want a baby, but is happy her body is shaping someone, who wants to go to paradise to have it, then give it away to a couple who can't have one, then go back to Spring fashions with a sense of accomplishment. It'll keep me sane having you on that jury, and maybe keep the jury sane."

"You're not mocking me?" she asked. He thought for a long time. Then he said to her, "Yes, I am. In a way. In a way, no. My daughter got rid of a pregnancy. You, you're one of the last of the innocents. You're like a fine rain in May." "I guess I am," she said, "you think I shouldn't play Eve?" "Play Eve," he said, "everybody else plays God." "Does Eve mean fool?" she asked him. "You have to be," he said. "The alternative is logic. This trial is about logic. I need a fool. If there was really no love, she's wrong. If there really was, he's wrong."

"Mine really wasn't love," she said to him. And there was a somber tone to her voice. "I don't accept that," he said. "Well, maybe a little," she said. She ran her hands along her thighs, then over her stomach. Then back to her thighs. She was inside herself again. "Well, maybe a lot more than I thought," she concluded. "Not for him, but for me." "I'll take any I can get," the judge said, "or we belong to hatred. And pay big bucks to belong." "You're shrewd," she said to him, "you've just tried my case! You want me to know what I love!" "I've tried mine, not yours," he said. "The day you walk in my courtroom with your own suit I'm guilty." "Of what?" she asked. "Of innocence," he said. "Whose?" she asked. "Mine," he answered.

Poor Butterfly

How happy are the poor in spirit;
theirs is the kingdom of heaven.
—Matthew 5:3

A girl loved butterflies. She had broken her leg chasing to see one, a black and white polka dot beauty. In the chase she put her foot in an old post hole and cracked her shin. She got back to the house on her own, she was ten, and the commotion there about getting her to the hospital was worse than the pain in her leg. Now here she was on the back porch with a cast on the leg, a cat in her lap, and a crazy laugh in her head about the whole event. As if one butterfly could turn the world into a table stacked with dishes, then tip the whole thing over in a crash that would make anyone laugh, never mind Bugs Bunny who did it at anything.

But what to do, immobilized, on the back porch, with family buzzing around her like yellow jackets? Family having never had anyone sick to take care of, except some broken-winged things and that only for a short while until they could get the creatures to a bird hospital. There was one a few miles away. She had seen the splinted hawks waiting their time until the hollow bones healed. And there was an owl she loved to watch, it could blink one eye at a time as if the other didn't exist. She had tried the same at table one night until her mother reached over, took her plate out onto the back porch, and brought it back with a dead mouse on it. She said, "Delicious! Cat just caught it. Was saving it for later. Poaching on owl territory though. You should scold it. Now eat, my darling."

"I want to *see* owl, not *eat* owl," the girl had said. She picked up the poor dead mouse by the tail, left her chair, and walked with the mouse dangling toward her brother seated on the other side of the table. He began to growl like a carnivore. He was a year older than she and knew things she

203

didn't. She stopped and walked towards her daddy who drew his napkin up in fright, as if drawing up bedclothes. She heard the cat at the screen door almost coming through like carrots through a strainer. So she went and dangled the mouse on her side of the screen. The cat turned into two eyes on a coiled spring whose tension she could feel. Quickly she opened the screen door and pitched the mouse to its fate. Her owl days ended right there.

And here was the cat in her lap. He loved the three quarters cast and would walk it to her bare ankle and foot then lick her toes until she giggled and twitched, then it would march back to her lap where it would curl itself into a sleeping ball. The butterfly landed on the railing a few feet from her. The same, the polka dot butterfly. She lifted the cat very quietly and dropped him beside the chair where he waited as he thought what to do. She lowered her leg from the deck chair and tried to stand without making a sound. But she had to stretch to do so, like someone doing splits in exercise class. She got upright, then edged along the railing to get closer to the beautiful little thing before it flew. Just as she got near, it did fly, not away, but toward her. And it landed on her nose. She didn't dare move. But it tickled her and she was cross-eyed trying to see it, and its wings were beating spasmodically as butterfly wings do. She couldn't focus, though it was right on her nose. "It will carry me away," she thought. "Like the man in the circus holding a rope in his teeth and swinging out and out and up and up!"

She heard a snap, a whirr, a chunk, her brother with the Polaroid camera, he had just shot her and the butterfly. Which flew up over her head. She turned as quickly as she could and saw the cat ready to leap after her butterfly. The cat was as cross-eyed as she trying to fix on the target. So she grabbed the cat's tail just as it leaped. She spun it through the air towards her brother, but he had ducked back inside and the cat hit the screen and held like a cliff climber until it could think what to do.

The butterfly was back on her shoulder before she noticed. Now she could look, turning her head very slowly to do so. She moved her shoulder slightly forward. There. A thrill went through her whole body. She could reach up and pinch hold of one of the wings and keep it. But she hated to see butterflies dead. Like that dumb painting, made from matched butterfly wings, of a battleship firing all its guns. She heard another snap, whirr, chunk, as her brother took a second shot. He had come back out very quietly. She saw the cat make an agile leap up onto the railing top and begin again its stalking walk towards her. When it got near enough, she reached out a friendly hand it wouldn't dodge then quickly shoved it overboard so it went into the bushes below scratching, screeching for a hold. The butterfly flew off and was gone. But there was an after-image on her eyes. She saw everything through butterfly wings for a few minutes before things returned to normal.

Her brother was roaring with laughter back inside the door looking at the photos he had taken. "Let me see!" she said. "Better not," he said. She knew he'd show it, so she said, "Well, don't!" "You'll rip it up," he said. "Promise I won't," she said. So he came out and said, "I hold it." "Okay," she said. And there she was in the photo looking cross-eyed like a comedienne at a butterfly on her nose. And her brother had caught the moment when the wings were spread widest. She burst out laughing, and she hobbled back toward the deck chair laughing, then crying until he just threw the photo at her like a frisbee because he saw she was really hurt. "Get me a scissors," she said to him. He picked up the photo. "It's too little," he said. "Well, maybe not. I got an idea." He went back in for the Polaroid. "Take another shot. Cut the butterfly out of this one, paste it on the new one." "No," she said, "let me keep it." "Okay," he said, "and keep this one too." It was a lovely shot of her face in profile looking down at the butterfly on her shoulder, again its wings spread beautifully showing the marvelous polka dot pattern. She felt she loved her own face as much as she loved the wings spread on the edge of her shoulder.

The cat was back up on her cast with a leap and a nosing at the back of the Polaroid shot for what it could yield. Her brother turned to look at the world for something to do next. The girl very slowly slid the comic shot in front of the gentle shot, saw again how silly she looked, then slid the gentle one in front of the comic one and saw how lovely she looked. Her brother had turned back towards her. She knew he saw the two sides of her showing on her face. He saw she loved those two sides. Just did. She held the two photos to her chest like finders keepers. He stood there with a feeling of accomplishment, then turned back toward the world to see what was next.

33rd Sunday, Ordinary Time

The Lesser of Two Evils

. . . you will not leave my soul among the
dead, nor let your beloved know decay.
—Psalm 16:10

"I didn't find him until ten years later. He was two when he was stolen."
A man was speaking. "My wife has been in a hospital for the last seven."
There was a murmur from the audience. "I left my son with the one who
had stolen him." The audience was stunned. All of them parents of miss-
ing children.

"I had tracked him down," the man continued. "But not until I figured
out who did it. An older woman who lived in the Cascades in Washington
state. Her son was in my platoon in Vietnam. I was good. I didn't lose
too many men. I fought a war not a movie. But there was this one scared
kid. I used to keep him back, never sent him on point. He used to study
the jungle like a botanist, not a soldier. Well, we had to be hauled out by
helicopter one day, we were surrounded. He fell off as we lifted and the
pilot wouldn't go back down. The kid got up and ran for us and was hit in
a second. I wrote to his mother, told her what happened and that it was
quick for him."

The man reached below the podium for a glass of water. "I told her I
was sorry." The man sipped some. "And I forgot about her and about the
war." He paused to think, then said, "Well, my wife and I had a child.
And I went into script writing for TV because I knew Vietnam stuff would
soon be in and World War II stuff would soon be out. 'Make a living off
your death,' a poet said. She killed herself the year I read the line. So I
had money, and we were happy, and the baby was on the back porch. The
front doorbell rang. My wife went to answer it. No one there. So she
went back to the porch and the baby was gone. She went screaming

around outside the house, then screaming in to phone the police, then me down at the studio. We live up in the hills, there's a drop behind our house through a grove of trees before you get to the next street. The baby simply disappeared, and no one had spotted anything suspicious. We tried everything. The milk carton photo, private investigators, every police network possible. And after three years my wife simply went into a depression and has not come back out of it."

The man sipped some more water. And looked around at the parents in front of him. "It took me a long time to figure out what had happened was not random. My baby was a boy, I said. I don't know what made the incident in Vietnam finally surface. When you're in hell you hear everything, not one thing. I sound cool now. But the only thing that kept me going was the thought that there had to be some sense. It was not like picking an apple off a tree. I actually thought that. Then thought where apples come from. Washington. Why Washington? Why that place in my head? The kid in Vietnam who loved to study the trees. A mother who lost a son. Oh! I said, it couldn't be! But it could. She was teaching me the loss of someone I loved. But she had moved many times in the intervening years. I searched everywhere in this old jeep I had. Three months here, then back to be with my wife. Then another three months. I lived on borrowed cash and did writing scrunched in the bucket seat using the steering wheel as a desk."

"Then I got the scent. There was a school teacher who lived up in a logging camp area who was bringing up her grandson. She was a botanist and the kid at thirteen was already an expert and winning prizes and trips, but she wouldn't let him accept the prizes and the trips because she didn't want him spoiled for the work, the work of conservation which would mean fighting the loggers and paper company instead of accepting their awards. I was in a store eating a sandwich and a coke and looking at a newspaper page with photo pinned to the bulletin board. I knew the boy's face, and the guy behind the counter told me more than he could ever guess."

I drove up to that camp. Like a scout, as unobtrusively as I could. Because I knew the boy was now part of a delicate eco-system himself. I had seen my wife break from a change in her system of love and trust. I did not want it to happen again because of me. I saw the woman. There was a school with several teachers who taught several subjects. A school made of logs that could become homes if they divided it up. She was really frail, though she looked tough, and was very intense, but intense about things outside her, not inside her, the way my wife is. She touched every growing thing she went by. She caressed a door before she entered it, her hand trailed on the log of a frame, or on the hair of a child passing by. The school was probably K through 9. And I saw him."

"He moved like her. I heard their voices and their voices were alike. And he seemed to have a thirst for life, he was always looking around him as if to check out the states of things. And he ran places. As if the air had to breathe him to stay alive. She had gotten a son back. I think I knew then that I would have to face her. But not face him. I would have to let her know I agreed and that someday she should tell him, when her own life was over, or when she had to let him go anyway."

"So I drove back to the nearest city and I found an Army/Navy store, and I bought a jungle outfit, helmet, boots. And I got a rifle and bayonet. Then drove back up the next day, put some broken branches in my helmet, went to the door of the school and stood there. But I stuck the rifle and bayonet in the ground and put the helmet on the butt. So when she came out she halted, looked at it, looked at me, and every ounce of blood drained out of her. That's when I turned and walked back to my jeep across the road. I started it up, put it in gear, but she ran in front of the jeep, put her hands on the hood as if to stop me. I have never seen a face so wild, not in war, not in love, not in anything.

"I turned the motor off. She came around to my side. I said, 'Sometime you tell him.' The blood rose back in her face. 'Meantime you killed.' I was weeping now. 'It has been too late for a long time,' she said, 'my hatred turned to love.' 'Sometime you tell him,' I said again, 'when you have to go or he does.' 'I will,' she said, and she stood back."

"She was filled with love at that minute. I could see it but it was like seeing through rain. So I drove away. And now I have to search for a way to get to the soul of my woman. With something that can change her into love. So all I have to say is if you do use intuition the way I suggest, be careful when you discover your lost child that you see what kind of system it is in. If you take it back into yours what will happen to it?"

"Meantime I need from you some wisdom. How do I reach a woman whose child has disappeared? I cannot tell her what I know, cannot tell her what judgment I have made. A judgment like those I used to make in combat. I don't seem to be enough myself. Do you know how to breed hope in a woman's soul? Thank you." He took another sip of water and stood down from the podium to where people could reach him.

The Feast of Christ the King

Intensive Care

I gazed into visions of the night.
—Daniel 7:3

"You know I was captured," a man was saying. "That war was so long ago!" He was talking to a nurse. "You might not remember it." She was watching his heartbeat in Intensive Care. "I learned about World War II in school," she said, "please be quiet." "It's pretty bad," he said, "I can feel it." "You won't feel it if you keep talking," she said. "I'm not afraid," he said, "I've been living on borrowed time." "Shhh," she said.

"I can see it again," he said. "We were at 35,000 feet. We took a hit. From a night fighter we never saw. I was navigator for the strike. Way south in Germany." "Please, sir, don't talk," the nurse said. "But I see that vision again," he said. "I know I'll be all right." She reached her hand and placed it very gently over his mouth. "Just see it," she said, "don't say it. I'm responsible." He laughed a bit into her palm. She lifted it. "Laughter's worse," she said and kept her hand hovering, then dropped it as she turned to go. The place was cluttered with equipment.

"My chute didn't open," he said very quietly through the oxygen hiss. She stopped. "Just partly," he went on. "A streamer. But it caught a tall tree. There was mud below from an early spring. Chute ripped. Branches did the rest. And the mud. I landed flat on my back in mud. Made like a cast in it. My breath was knocked out. I remember that first breath after. It was pure life. And as sweet as this oxygen. I got up like a miracle. And I sat against that tree until morning came. Like in a trance. I saw in the morning light my own shape in the mud and it had filled with water. Like I had just been fashioned by God then lifted out of the cast. It's like what I feel now."

"Sir," the nurse said, "you're heart is not coming out intact from this. Maybe not coming out at all if you pressure it this way." He smiled. "I've been dead for forty-five years," he said. She shook her head. "Mysticism later. My father was one of you." She had come back to the side of the bed. "He had a spent 88 shell land in his lap. He was eating a tin of corned beef in a barn in Normandy and a shell went through a thick tree, tore up some ground, went through a manure pile, plucked a few chickens, then into the barn, through a beam and plop, into his lap. He would illustrate holding my brother's football. He had visions of himself splattered all over the Norman countryside. Then he'd go through the joke again. Man dies. Man decomposes in ground. Ground becomes grass. Grass becomes cow. Cow becomes meat. Meat becomes meal. You might be eating great grandpa, kiddoes. So we often couldn't eat."

"How did he know about that shell?" the man asked. She put her hand over his mouth again. "He crawled out of the barn and traced the furrow and spotted the gun and shot the gunners and wore the medal later even to bed." There were some tears on the man's face now. Running into the nurse's hand. She lifted it and with her fingers wiped the wetness away. "I loved him," she said. "As much as he could be loved." Her patient was now still. But he said, "I'm not one of those." "I'm glad," she said. She turned to go. "You probably could be loved more." "I was," he said. "Don't be afraid to pull the plug. They won't want to. Especially my wife. But don't you be afraid." "If you keep talking they'll never get to see you," she said, "now shush."

"God just peeled me from the ground like a wet leaf," he said. "Then walked me out to a road right into a Nazi patrol. And I had this beatific look on my face, I guess. So they didn't bash me. Just put me away. Even now, do you see, I'm happy. I'm so happy. Everything is so . . . your hand, your voice, your old clunk of a father. That blip I can see, it's a drunk who can't climb the stairs. He's got his shoes off not to wake his wife and is bunging his toes and he'll ring the doorbell." She put her hand back over his mouth. "Then I'll have to stand here," she said, "or you'll be a happy corpse."

There was a slight laughter in the man. "You're right with yourself," she said. "So think care, think delicacy with this body. Whatever knitting it can do it will. And if you're happy, just let the happiness rise, but don't tell

212 All Eyes and Blind

me, I can see it, and see it on the machine. Your wife's outside. I have to keep her at bay. She's like popcorn hitting the lid." He smiled under her hand. "Your children have been phoned for." He kissed her palm. She lifted it cautiously. "Arf," he said. She drew it away entirely. Looked at the monitor. Then at the tubes. "I've been a gardener since. Architect. Landscapes." He spoke quickly, then pressed his lips together. Before she could stop him.

She knew if she left he'd stop. So she did, and pulled the curtains a bit. She could see and not be seen. And hear what he said. "It's man dies. Man decomposes. Man recomposes. Into grass. Into brooks. Into dragonflies. Into willows weeping over brooks. Into carp. Into babies' bottoms and women's breasts and men's biceps and rolling in the grass, rolling and rolling, until they can't breathe, and it all disappears. Blip, blip's no good. You listening?"

"Yes," she said, coming back. "You won't let me not." "He dead?" the man asked. She thought whether to answer, checked monitor, tubes, oxygen level. "He is," the man said for her. Some tears sprang to her eyes. "You don't scare," she said. "He drank. The shell landed in his lap again, at the end. The DT's. He didn't know where to run." "Ah," the man said, "God rest him." "Yes," she said, "rest." She was now standing next to the bed. "I hope rest does it. Meantime you. Not another peep. So we peel you like a leaf soon. Out of that bed. Then back into captivity. But you have nice guards this time. She adores you. Sorry about the popcorn." "Soda water," he said, "but she never loses her fizz. You see him out?" "Yes," she answered. "Like this?" "The opposite," she said. "That's why you let me talk, right?" She couldn't speak. Almost not see. "It's in my lap, okay?" he said. "Okay," she said, "now just count blips and sleep. Over the fence, one, two." "They're nipples," he said, "trying to escape. Need help. One, two."

King Kong Eats Flowers

Because the world refused to acknowlege
him, therefore it does not acknowlege us.
—1 John 3:1

"My father was a clown," a woman was saying. The talk show host just let her talk. "A real clown—circus, theater, church sometimes. When I was a kid I loved him for it. When I was a teenager I hated him. I told my mother that and I think she hated me for a while. So they sent me to prep school and told me to say he was in media. I didn't see him often. But once my roommates were in New York and so was the circus. They went to it and found out the clown was my Dad. Or they knew before and went to see.

He was good. He was great in fact. By that time he had become a mock circus. He did fantastic imitations of the high bar people. And he did it high. His pants would come off and float down and he'd swoop after, catch them, then try to put them on while going back and forth. My roommates were all over the bed and chairs trying to show me. And he did this lion thing in the cage with no tamer, just himself in a clown suit and lion's head, through the fire ring and splat, falling off the stand and chasing his lion's head around, trying to pull one off a real lion until the lion roared and he scatted up the bars. Then his lion head would float serenely by on a string while the real lions crouched below ready to eat him. And so on and so on.

They were all over me, my three roommates. And I was more and more mortified until I just burst out crying. I loved him so much and that clown life burned me, I didn't want to hear of it, yet I was ashamed of being caught out that way. They didn't bring him up again, we were really friends, but they treated me as kind of sacred, they had never been in such

213

a human struggle before, genius clown's daughter crushed by clown's role, seeks life of her own. They were rich and bored. So they wanted more of this dramatic struggle. They went beyond friendship into curiosity.

They got the headmaster to invite my father as a surprise to our Halloween party. We have a hall we use as a basketball court and a banquet place and a theater for plays and musicals. It's what we set up for Halloween and invite a boy's school over plus a lot of parents and it does get crazy in a stiff kind of way. People come dressed as J.P. Morgan and King Tut. Well, right in the middle of it a man with a pumpkin head on and a butterfly net in one hand appears overhead on one of the beams that cross the space, like the crosspiece of an A. And several butterflies start to fly through the air. The pumpkin head is standing trying to catch the butterflies and he leans, starts to teeter, regains balance, starts to lean back, teeters, it was fantastic, I don't know how he got to make those butterflies move. Then his pumpkin head falls off, but it too starts to swing around, and the man has no head. He makes a terrific grab for his head and his arm comes off right at the socket and starts to swing around all by itself and go after the pumpkin head. Then he reaches out with the other arm, it comes out of its socket, it floats through the air, how I don't know. So the headless, armless man reaches out with one leg to try and catch the other members, and the leg comes off and starts to swing through the air with the rest. Then, my God, he starts to hop up in the air on the one leg, up off the beam, and tries to kick his pumpkin head back but can't and lands back on the beam where he does the teeter-totter again. Everybody going ooh! aah! So he jumps again, hooks his head with his leg, kicks it towards him, lands back on the beam just as his head sails in on his shoulders and he's a pumpkin head again. Then he leans way out and bites an arm and brings it in, on it goes. The arm catches the arm that's still swinging, puts it back on. The two arms catch the other leg, put it back on. Then the pumpkin man throws his arms up for applause. Everybody applauds. The pumpkin man then walks right across the air to the balcony rail, turns, bows again, and disappears.

We were all holding our breaths, he was so good. All done with wires we knew, but what an illusion of no wires! I knew he was a genius. He came to join the rest of the party wearing his pumpkin head, then took it off. They saw how small he really was which enabled him to work inside a dummy. I was taller than he, like my mother. He sensed that I was embarrassed. People treated us both like circus. And he kept it up. He balanced a champagne glass on his nose before he drank it. He was pulling coins out of his ears, dropping them, looking for them, they would then drop out of his hair as he bent and he'd catch them in the palm of his hand, all the while talking about something else to my friends and their parents. I finally ran and my friends loved this deep novel going on right before their eyes, far better than the clown act up in the rafters. He didn't come out after me. Instead he walked on his hands over to the food table, took a glass of cider with his feet, drank it using his feet as hands, then walked out the door, they told me, got in his car and left.

What they didn't know was that I had learned many of his tricks during the time I adored him. So I decided to give them a show every day if I could. Just out of revenge. One day in dining hall I needed some tongue—ugh! tongue and spinach!—from the other end of the table. So I got up, stood on my hands at the end, walked down the center, took a slice of tongue in my mouth, then walked on my hands back to my place. I had on black panties and had sewn two pink hands around the fanny part as if someone were feeling me. The place roared, but roared with embarrassment. Well, I was forgiven that one. But not the one in chapel.

It was my turn one day to go up to the Bible stand, open the huge text to the day's passage, then read it. Well, I got a cardboard box and shaped it like a Bible, painted it as one does in the theater. Then I bought a lot of parakeets. And just before chapel I put the parakeets in the fake Bible. There were holes to let in air. I went in and put it in the place of the real Bible, put the real one behind some copes in the sacristy. Then, an hour later, chapel started, hymn first, oration second, then the nod to me to come read from the Bible. I went up in a very dignified way, stepped to the podium behind the bookstand, intoned in my fourteen year old voice, 'A reading from Revelations.' I opened the fake Bible and my parakeets shot out and up into the air and started to zoom all over the place. And I started to chase them up around the altar doing all the classic tumbles and pratfalls my father had taught me as if sincerely trying to catch the little things and restore order to the solemn ceremony. This time I had on white panties under my uniform skirt. I had sewn red flames on it, rising from the thighs up to the waist, hot pants. And they flashed every time I tumbled down the steps or went reaching in over a choir stall until one of the teachers finally grabbed me, she taught us English, and my sweater came away and I had this body stocking on with King Kong's face on it and he eating a flower. Well the howl in the chapel was like the howl of hell it was so hysterical. So I jumped to the head of the aisle and somersaulted my way right down and out of the chapel.

I packed to go. And I saw they loved me again, my roommates. And I saw it was because I had created another reality. Not a clown reality. But a liberty, one that gave them astonishing joy, a moment of utter freedom that ruined nothing. They kissed me into a damp rag.

So I went back to him. I got a mannekin's head and a wig. Then I made a cage to hide my upper body in, my head below the collar bone. I held my mannekin head in my hands and I knocked on his dressing room door. He opened it. He knew my sweater. And my head in my hands. He screamed like a woman at a mouse and jumped up in my arms, his arms around my no head shoulders, "Save me, save me," he said. My cage gave way and we both ended on the floor. "They phoned me," he said. "You're a blasphemer. I'm to punish you." "I'm a clown," I said as I pulled the cage off me. "Punishment enough," he said. I've been one since.

Breech Births

Wait and see if Elijah will come to
take him down . . .
—Mark 15:36

"I don't know what they'll charge me with, what you'll charge me with. But I'd do it again." A man was speaking. To his son, but he did not say son. There was anger and disbelief in the son. He was seeing his father in a hospital room that was under police guard. "Your grandmother had the same kind of cancer," the father said. "She died like a tortured animal. And your mother saw no sense to the same for her. And I am not going to live without your mother. So you better keep me locked up." His voice was quivering. It was from age as well as ordeal. Eighty years can shake a voice.

"No, I get to take you home," the son said. "I get to take home a suicide who survived. I'd rather take her home. Too bad you floated and she didn't." "Just leave the window open and go talk to the cop," the father said. "Nice," said the son. "Then *I'd* be up on charges. Like you." "You were always afraid," the father said, almost talking to himself. "I always had something to lose," the son said, "you never did. Until now maybe. Then you were afraid. Afraid to go on. You're afraid to go on." There was nothing left to say.

"Get these tubes out of me," the father said. His hands were tied in bandages to the side of the bed. "They'll be out soon," the son said, "soon as pneumonia's not a risk." "You ever see an animal die?" the father said. "Yes," the son said, "in a bullfight. In Spain. When I was with the Air Force." "Okay, that was your mother, and the bullfighter was cancer, and I was goddamned if I'd let it happen." "Jesus, Dad," the son said, "don't you understand we're not animals, we can make sense of things! You have to

217

turn it into a farce. A bullfight would have been noble. Two old skeletons in a canoe right down the middle of the Niagara River, standing, naked, like a bride and groom from Halloween, then over the lip of the Falls with all the real brides and grooms watching in horror! And screaming up to the hotel to get the police! And she drowns and you don't! And I get called to come lug home a corpse and a criminal! I really ought to be laughing my frigging head off. I never liked you. I loved her. But I always respected you. You were cold but you had brains. You've got mush now!" The son got up from his chair and walked between the walls to let his emotions calm.

"I could feel the wind on my skin. I could feel her shiver with it too. And we had to balance in that canoe, balance each other, it was delicate, like the first time I loved her, before I left for Guadalcanal. There was strength in that water, not this drip, drip you can count like an insomniac. And the roar of death, it was nature roaring, not a shell screeching. And we went over the right spot. And she was torn from me, torn from me the right way, in a plunge of water, a roil of water. Then it spat me out. Okay, I'm no good I said, you only take the good. But I went through that door with her. Someone shoved me back out and slammed it in my face. But I went through that door with her. Wherever she goes I go." The father's voice was fierce for all its frailty.

"So I tell them you'll do it again," the son said, now standing at the window. "Then they say not over our Falls. Get a bridge somewhere. Why didn't you do it at home? God, they're as cold as rifle butts too."

"We saw this on our honeymoon," the old man said. This time his voice was very distant, a long way back in time. The son came to the bed again and looked at his father. "But then it was a woman only. And not a canoe. It was like a surfboard. And she was young. Like a Rhinemaiden. And her fiance' had been killed at Dunquerque. We read in the paper the next day. And she was flat on that board until she reached the lip. Then she stood and was gone. And that's what your mother remembered when she got the verdict from the doctor. She wanted to go alone. But I refused unless she took me."

"It is Grand Opera," the son said. Then he went on, "I'm not afraid of death. I'm afraid of what it does to people. That's why I left the service. We used to fly those planes at one another as if we'd spit death right in the face. So we'd blow up anything if they told us. Shoot anything if they told us. I saw you look at me when I came out. You have that same spit. Except your lungs are weak." "That bullfight," the father said, "remember it. That bull is your mother. You can't stop what you see."

"It shows me once again," the son said, "you know nothing about love. And maybe she didn't either. And that Rhinemaiden. She just left a barren space for somebody else to live in." The son's knuckles were up to his mouth. "Love goes out with people a different way. And those who go out, they can create a life, except nobody tells them, nobody says they can defeat horror, they can leave living souls behind. It's too much for a human to think that."

"Christ, you don't even have skirts," the father said and started to cough. It took him some time to settle. The son had to hold a phlegm bowl while he spat out. "Love is stronger than death, old man," the son said very calmly. "It flew right at you and you flinched. It's flying right at you now. But you don't want to see if it is. She didn't either. You were well matched. Well, I'm going to find out."

"I'll show you," the father said, "I'll show you again. Just get me to that window. She's waiting." He started to tug at his restraints. Then he started to cough. This time he spat by himself, on the floor. "That's what you leave behind," the son said. "Someone has to scrape it up. Sputum. Or your corpse out the window. Like scum. Or drag you out by the hind hooves and you leave a trail of blood. Or you can leave love intact. Not covered with spit. Not covered with scum."

"Whose love?" the father said. "You never loved me." "I never did," the son said, "I don't now. But I'm the only one standing here. And I'm flying right at you. And I'm not going to pull up." "What am I to tell you?" the father asked. "You're to tell me why you can't live without her. You're to tell me its love. And you're to mean it. And if you mean it, I open that window and I throw you out. So you don't have to stink this world up anymore." "Grand opera," the father said and did some more coughing, "so who's kidding whom?" "Okay," the son said, "don't say a thing." He walked to the window and opened it. Then went to the bedside and untied the restraints. Pulled out the needle in the father's arm. "She's just outside that window," he said, "the woman you love. You'll get her back for sure when you hit the ground."

The father didn't move. He stared at his son, fearlessly. "You were a breech birth," he said, "came out ass first." "Out of whom?" the son asked back. "They had to cut her," he said, "I saw later." "Who?" the son said. "So we cut first for your sisters," the father went on, "you all lead with your asses." "She have a good one?" the son asked. "Yes," the father said. "I'm chilly. Close that window."